A Family LOVE STORY

Lou Beardsley

Harvest House Publishers
Irvine, California 92714

A Family
LOVE STORY

A FAMILY LOVE STORY

Copyright © 1975 Harvest House Publishers
Irvine, California 92714
Library of Congress Catalog Card Number: 75-37095
ISBN - 0 - 89081-017-6

Printed in the United States of America

*This book is dedicated
to my own "family love story" . . .
George, Jeff, Jay, Nancy and Gary.*

INDEX

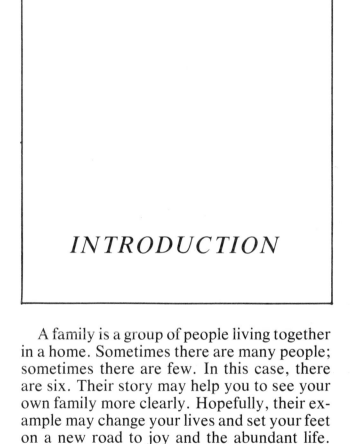

INTRODUCTION

A family is a group of people living together in a home. Sometimes there are many people; sometimes there are few. In this case, there are six. Their story may help you to see your own family more clearly. Hopefully, their example may change your lives and set your feet on a new road to joy and the abundant life. There may be trials and disappointments, but in James we are told to expect trials, because they test our faith, and produce endurance so that we may be perfect and complete, lacking in nothing! When you are following God's plan for your family, you needn't fear the future for your children. *He will both precede and follow you, and lay His hand of blessing upon your head.* (Psalms 139:5)

Though you and your family are living together in the same house, related, loving, and dependent upon each other, you are all different. Your reactions to circumstances are different, your goals are diversified, and your likes and dislikes may vary a great deal. This all adds up to problems and disagreements among you. This is to be expected. If no one in your family has ever had a disagreement or a cross word, we'd like to meet you . . . you could teach us a few things!

The family in this book is a real family. In fact, it is a composite of many real families, and the situations are real life situations. However, the names have been changed to protect the innocent (and the guilty). We hope you will be able to identify with the members of the Johnson family . . . that you will profit by their mistakes and gain by their experiences. The most important fact about them is that they are Christians . . . "Christ-ones." They belong to the Lord Jesus Christ by the simple fact that they have all invited Him to come into their hearts and make His home there, and to take over their lives. (In varying degrees, of course . . . some are following Him more closely than others and are reaping the benefits. Others need to make a more firm commitment to Him.) Real family love without the Lord is impossible. *Except the Lord build the house, they labor in vain that build it.* (Psalms 127:1) Jesus Christ is the cornerstone . . . the foundation to our faith, the Key that unlocks the door to heaven and the personality Who unites our family and makes us "one in the bond of love!"

1

There's One
In Every Family

The Johnson family was in their back yard, about to experience a dream come true. They had saved enough money to have a swimming pool installed. It was finally filled with water, and Jim Johnson had lined up his four children and explained that they would all jump in at the same time! No "going first" and no "favorites." Tommy, 14, was blond, handsome, and serious. He was very athletic and a good student. Although he was shy, he had many friends. Mike, 12, was the complete opposite in disposition of his brother. Dark hair, dark eyes, as outgoing as Tommy was shy, and not particularly interested in either sports or school. Cars were his "thing" and he spent hours building soapbox models and reading "Hot Rod" magazine. Lynn, 11, was petite, blond and a charmer. Popular and social, she was always president of everything, and kept her parents busy driving her to dancing school, Brownies, piano lessons and Sunday school activities. Scott, 9 years old, was already showing signs of becoming the family "clown." Gifted musically, he was constantly playing the guitar, piano or any other instrument that was handy, doing imitations, writing songs, and driving the entire family crazy with his forgetfulness.

As Jim Johnson explained how he would count "1, 2, 3, *jump*" when it was time to get into the pool, his wife Nancy watched from the end of the pool deck. "Okay now . . . here we go . . . One . . . two . . . SPLASH!" A gasp of indignation came from the other three children as Mike leaped into the water ahead of the count, and suddenly all four of them were splashing around. The eyes of their parents met and they shook their heads, disappointed in their second son, but unwilling to spoil this special day by insisting he get out of the water and go to his room.

S.O.S. Means Save Our Sanity

Maybe you can identify with Jim and Nancy Johnson. You may not have four children or a swimming pool, but chances are you have a "Mike" in your family. We've found very few homes that didn't have one. (She may be a female . . . this personality type doesn't necessarily run to boys!) In each home, however, the question is the same: What can we do?

Mike had the looks and personality of one who could sell home freezers to Eskimos. His "gift of gab" would wear anyone down and he handled the truth rather loosely. Although professing to faith in Jesus Christ, his life did not exhibit the "fruits of the Spirit." At church, he was known as the teacher's trial, interrupting at just the right (or wrong) moment to spoil the climax of the lesson. He gave the assistant pastor's son a black eye in class one day, and as he progressed into his teens, his wisecracks broke up many a class and broke the heart of many a teacher.

In school he was constantly getting into mischief, beginning with practical jokes on the teachers and later on, cutting classes, and finally, cutting school. It was extremely hard for authorities to punish him because he turned on the charm to justify his misdeeds, or if that wasn't possible, "sweet-talk" his way out of trouble. Loaded with talent and potential, many teachers took a special interest in the challenge of trying to help him to mature enough to develop into a responsible citizen, only to realize as he went on his merry way that "they'd been had!"

Down With Debate

From experience let me suggest, the first point to remember when dealing with the "Mike" of your family is: *Don't Argue!*

Mike is a master of the art of oral self-defense, and if you attempt to reason or argue with him, he will have you so confused that *you* may even end up apologizing to *him*! When punishment is due, listen to his side, state your case and the punishment with no further discussion.

The second point to remember is: *Be sure to follow through!*

Let's Not Make a Deal

Mike had a clever way of talking his parents into a lesser punishment than that originally declared. For instance, they had grounded him for the weekend for leaving the house for the evening without permission. After a couple of hours, he appeared, very docilely, and requested permission to speak to his father.

He had a proposal which, he explained, would be very beneficial to them both. It would fulfill his punishment and at the same time accomplish a job that needed to be done around the house. He would weed the entire back yard . . . all the flower and vegetable gardens, in return for having his "grounding" lifted. He would work the entire weekend, both days if necessary, to finish the job.

Eyeing the weeds with one eye and his golf clubs with the other, Jim Johnson succumbed to the temptation. "As long as he's punished, it doesn't really matter which method" he thought to himself. "Okay, it's a deal," Jim answered. Mike gleefully ran outside and began pulling weeds with all the speed he could muster. A couple of hours after his dad had left for the golf course, he appeared triumphantly to his mother and announced that the job was done. She shook her head in disbelief, but upon inspecting the yard, had to admit he was right. What she didn't realize was Mike's resourcefulness. In true "Huck Finn" fashion, he had hired Lynn and Scott for a quarter each to help him, swearing them to silence and taking a chance that his mother, busy with her sewing, would not observe the two younger children working in a secluded spot invisible from the house.

This accomplished three things. First, it

proved to Mike that he could change his parents' minds. Secondly, he found that through his own ingenuity, he could escape real punishment. The third result was that it established a pattern. Never again would Mike settle for a punishment without trying to make a deal with his parents, teachers or future employers. He would use this same play over and over in different situations for years to come, always escaping the consequences of his actions. Mike's problem was rationalization. He would not face up to his own wrong doing, he would always justify it. He wasn't sorry for his mischief . . . he was only sorry he got caught.

Choose His Chums

Another very important point in dealing with Mike is to carefully supervise his choice of friends. His outgoing personality and leadership qualities will attract a group of weak-willed "followers" who will pull him down scholastically, morally and spiritually. He tends to avoid the strong Christian kids because they refuse to go along with his plans and ideas for what he calls "fun." If he begins to form friendships with kids you find hard to communicate with, or those who seem almost too "polite" in their actions toward you, encourage him not to see them. If he's younger than teens or under driving age, this will be easier to do, but if he's over 15, it will require effort and very close supervision on your part.

The Johnsons failed in this area when they were swayed by Mike's argument that these boys his parents felt negatively about were from poor environments and that the Johnson home was the only Christian home to which they had access. They realized later that when the boys refused their invitation to church, they should have discouraged the friendships to progress further. Later on, when Scott was a freshman in high school and began bringing home non-Christian friends whose parents had different standards than theirs, Jim and Nancy insisted he break off close relations with them. When he was not allowed to participate in their off-campus activities, he began associating with his former friends, who were Christians, and it changed the course of his life.

Pray For Pointers

Remember to pray for God's direction in handling a difficult child. Ask for His wisdom to know when your youngster is engaged in a wrongdoing (James 1:5). This is helpful in dealing with children who sneak to disobey their parents. The boy who crawls out the bedroom window after his parents are asleep or the girl who meets her boyfriend secretly while on a trip to the library can go undetected unless you seek God's wisdom. If you pray for God to reveal your children's dis-obedience to you so that you can train them in His ways, He will be faithful to do so. He will awaken you late at night with a reason to enter the room of the "window-crawler-outer," as he did the Johnsons. Or a friend will mention having seen your daughter and her boyfriend on the night she was supposed to have been at the library, as in the case of the Johnson's neighbors.

When you discover that your children have lied or been dishonest with you, it is necessary for you and your husband to decide before-hand what the punishment should be. (Dad should make the final decision.) A meeting between the three of you in the privacy of your bedroom would be best. Parents should begin by praying aloud for understanding, but not forcing the young person to pray. This type of child may not be committed to the Lord, or perhaps not be a Christian at all; or he may just be too emotionally upset to pray out loud. Look up Scriptures beforehand that refer to lying, disrespect of parents, cheating, immo-rality, or whatever the offense was. (A topical Bible is invaluable if you are not a walking Biblical encyclopedia.) Read these Scriptures which fit the situation to your child and ask him if he understands how his misdeed is contrary to God's will. This is a good beginning, but if he or she rebels at this idea, explain that God instructs us as parents to discipline our children and that you want God's best for him; therefore, the punishment will be a spanking with a rod—in the case of a younger child—or a restriction such as grounding, no use of the car for a period of time, no phonograph or TV, etc. for the teenager. Be sure that the punishment fits the crime. It is important that you be fair, and sneaking out the window obviously deserves a more severe punishment than being late for dinner.

Your "Mike" probably has more potential for serving the Lord and being successful than the other children in your family because of his ingenuity, resourcefulness, charm and intelligence. These same traits, when channeled in the wrong direction, can lead to disaster and heartache.

Jim Johnson remarked thoughtfully one evening to close friends, "God gave us Mike to keep us on our knees and humble. Never again will I criticize another person's effort (or lack of it) in raising his family. If all of our children were easy to deal with, we would become complacent and lack compassion for others with problems."

2

Four Kids:
Four Temperaments

"Both of our kids are different from each other!" remarked a neighbor of Nancy Johnson's over coffee. "We have four and they're *all* as different as night and day," replied Nancy. "Each one reacts differently to a given situation and they each have their own friends, tastes, interests and goals."

No Two Alike

God created each of us individually. No two of us are alike. Even identical twins are different in personality. Our main differences lie in our temperaments. Each of us has various degrees of two or more of the four basic temperaments in our make-up. The four temperaments are: sanguine, choleric, melancholy and phlegmatic. (See following page for temperament characteristics.)

Normally each of us is predominately one temperament with one or more of the others in either strengths or weaknesses. To discern your temperament check your strengths and weaknesses under each of the four categories. The one with the most checks is your basic temperament. You know your children better than anyone else does, so you can go through the chart and pretty well determine them. This will be invaluable in discerning how to motivate and channel their energies. Each child needs specific training in order to function as God intended. Part of our job description as parents is to equip our child to fulfill his mission here on earth as part of the body of Christ.

In *The Fulfilled Woman* we explained the basic temperaments by doing thumbnail sketches of each predominant one. Tim LaHaye covers them in much more detail in his book, *Spirit Controlled Temperament.*

The Johnson children were four in number and four in temperament. Tommy was a melancholy with a large amount of phlegmatic. Mike, choleric with sanguine; Lynn was sanguine with a mixture of choleric and melancholy, while Scott was a phlegmatic with lesser degrees of sanguine. No wonder they were so different!

The Four Temperaments

Strengths	*Weaknesses*
Sanguine	
Personable	Undependable
Optimistic	Procrastination
Enthusiastic	Fearful
Warm	Exaggerates
Friendly	Undisciplined
Compassionate	Unstable
Talkative	Weak-willed
Warm	Egocentric
Carefree	Loud
Outgoing	Restless
	Emotional
	Forgetful

Choleric

Confident	Proud
Optimistic	Angry
Independent	Cruel
Leader	Sarcastic
Practical	Domineering
Productive	Self-sufficient
Resourceful	Unemotional
Strong-willed	Sly
Determined	Inconsiderate
Decisive	Stubborn
Fearless	

Melancholy

Sensitive	Moody
Perfectionist	Fearful
Gifted	Pessimistic
Analytical	Critical
Idealistic	Unsociable
Aesthetic	Negative
Self-sacrificing	Self-centered
Loyal	Theoretical
	Revengeful
	Rigid

Phlegmatic

Dependable	Stingy
Calm	Fearful
Efficient	Indecisive
Conservative	Unmotivated
Easy-going	Selfish
Practical	Self-protective
Humorous	Spectator
Diplomat	Lazy
Leader	

Tranquil Tom

Tommy was the easiest to deal with, having mainly the temperament strengths of the melancholy with a balance of many of the phlegmatic strengths, and his weaknesses lay mostly in the phlegmatic area. In the melancholy realm, he was sensitive, a perfectionist, gifted, analytical, idealistic, self-sacrificing and loyal. His spiritual gift was mercy and he always had a ready ear for a friend with a problem. His room was neat as a pin with a place for everything and everything in its place. Very athletic, he was still a talented poet, adept at literature and mathematics. He was a trifle moody but had none of the more devastating of the melancholy traits which his sister possessed. His temperament weaknesses lay in the phlegmatic column . . . unmotivated, a spectator, with a bit of laziness thrown in. Even though he was extremely well coordinated, he lacked the push to be outstanding in athletics until his senior year in high school. At batting practice, he would take his place at the end of the line and if time ran out before his turn came up, he never complained. At basketball, he passed the ball to the other boys to make the shots, and at football he was unaggressive until as a senior, a discerning coach saw a potential and took the time to develop it to the point where his accurate pass receiving and running helped to make a championship team that year. With leadership qualities, he was a follower until he became Spirit-filled after he was married and had a son of his own.

Maddening Mike

Mike was the typical outgoing choleric, but with the problem of many sanguine weaknesses. He was very confident, optimistic, independent, resourceful and determined, and he was usually the leader (or instigator) in his crowd. On the negative side of the choleric ledger, he was very sly and also quite inconsiderate. His sanguine traits came out in his personable, enthusiastic, carefree and talkative personality. Most of his weaknesses were in the sanguine area . . . he was undisciplined, restless, egocentric and prone to exaggeration. His complete commitment to the Lord didn't take place until adulthood and he was the reason for more than one gray hair for his parents. His spiritual gift was leadership, but this did not develop until he became Spirit-filled.

Loquacious Lynn

Lynn was the typical popular sanguine girl, but with some of the choleric leadership qual-

ities that made it difficult for her to be submissive to the male sex. Her melancholy traits
were a source of frustration to her parents
because most of those were on the negative
side. She was personable, enthusiastic, warm,
friendly, compassionate, talkative, and
outgoing . . . a typical sanguine who sparks
up any room with a mere appearance. She was
prone to exaggeration however, though most
of hers, unlike her brother Mike's, was simply
a desire to make a good story and involved
little slyness or guile. On the choleric side, she
was practical, productive, resourceful,
strong-willed, determined, and anger-prone.
Fortunately when she was grown, God
brought her a choleric-phlegmatic husband
who was stronger than she in these areas, and
to whom she could be submissive. Her melancholy self-sacrificing and sensitivity made her
commitment to the Lord come at a very early
age. Her spiritual gift was service and God
was able to use her greatly even in her teen
years. This same melancholy was a source of
extreme frustration to her parents because of
her negativism and self-critical and pessimis-
tic outlook. Although possessing unusual
physical attractiveness, she was so critical
that she lacked self-confidence and was often
found sobbing in her room because of the
imagined ugliness and preoccupation with her
weight, which never progressed beyond a size

seven dress! Even her popularity, abundance of dates and election to homecoming queen in high school failed to boost her ego enough to overcome this negative self-image. Only the sensitivity of her husband was able to raise her opinion of herself and overcome her imbalance in this area.

Slothful Scott

Scott was the family master-of-ceremonies. His phlegmatic sense of humor broke the ice in many a tense situation and resulted in a burst of laughter. He was calm, easy-going, humorous and conservative; but on the negative side, was unmotivated, lazy and a procrastinator, combined with the sanguine forgetfulness and lack of self-discipline. These traits caused his unusually gifted musical talents to be unused to their full potential until he was out of his teen years. All of the sanguine strengths were his, and combined with the spiritual gift of exhortation, made him a very effective witness for Christ after his firm commitment at the end of his junior year in high school. However, his undependability, procrastination, forgetfulness and undisciplined life-style prevented his being used to his full potential until he reached adulthood. If he was sent on an errand, he would meet a friend, begin witnessing to him, and forget all about the errand.

As a youngster, his locker at school was full of forgotten sweaters, jackets, books, athletic equipment and musical instruments needed at home. As a young adult, he would promise to teach a Sunday school class and do a musical number for the worship service at the same hour in church, not realizing his mistake until the last moment. This resulted in many frustrating moments for those who were depending upon him, but his warm personality and sense of humor got him through many a hairy situation and prevented the loss of friends usually resulting from this kind of forgetfulness. His parents took a firm position in insisting he keep a list of his activities (commitments, and chores) tacked up in a conspicuous place in his bedroom. As he became more and more Spirit-controlled, these undesirable traits lessened, but the need for the notes persisted!

Note The Needs

Your children probably aren't exactly the same temperaments as any of the Johnson children, but you will undoubtedly recognize many of their traits in yours. Tommy's great need was for encouragement. Always a good student, his spectator qualities and poor self-image had to be erased by compliments from his parents, and a tireless effort on the part of his father to develop his abilities in the athletic area. Hours were spent "catching" for him as he perfected his pitching. His tendency to expect perfection of himself made him a joy to have in a classroom, but he had to be encouraged greatly to participate in sports and other activities because of his fear that he would not be good enough. His sense of humor made him fun to be with and when he was given a job to do, he did it with all the dependability and efficiency of the melancholy. The Johnsons often remarked, kiddingly, that if they hadn't had Tommy first, they might not have gone on to the other three children!

Mike, as difficult to deal with as his brother was easy, refused to fit into any mold. When his parents thought they had the answer to his personality problems and he seemed to be committing his life to Christ, he would do an about-face and backslide to the point where they wondered if he was a believer at all! His problem, particularly as he got into his teens and twenties, was holding onto the world with one hand and God with the other. Unwilling to completely dedicate himself to one or the other, he was successful at neither and constantly searching for contentment until he let go of the world. He was well into his twenties before this occurred, and caused his parents many a heartache in his determined effort to find his niche through worldly success and material gain.

Discipline Is Dandy

Mike's need was a firm hand of discipline, a follow-through of every punishment, and a breaking of the will without breaking his spirit. His parents were unprepared for him after their firstborn, who was sensitive to their instruction and respectful of their wishes. Tom had a high regard for authority, and a keen spiritual inclination, which seemed completely lacking in Mike. This is fairly typical of second children, according to the Institute in Basic Youth Conflicts. If the older child is interested in spiritual things, the younger will go in the opposite direction, and vice versa. In retrospect, the Johnsons realized that they needed to spend more time with Mike, seeking to develop his qualities in a more positive direction, and to be more firm in the area of discipline.

Lynn, like her oldest brother, was easier on her parents. The most difficult area in her life was her melancholy pessimism. This type of child needs boosting and encouragement to overcome the self-pity. If she is possessed with a sense of humor (which Lynn was) it's easier to "kid" them out of their depression. If they don't have this humor, a firm hand is needed plus a large quantity of Scripture memorization to help them over the rough spots. A girl with several choleric traits must be encouraged to see the value of submissiveness to a future husband. If she marries a phlegmatic, she may run roughshod over him and take the family leadership completely out of his hands. The sanguine needs prodding to follow through on his activities, and also warning not to take on too much. Their desire to please makes them easy targets for saying "yes" to everything that is asked of them, and getting so bogged down with so many responsibilities they are unable to do any of them well.

Laugh Or You'll Cry

If you have a "Scott," we hope you are also possessed with a sense of humor. Otherwise, his forgetfulness will become so frustrating you will have a problem holding your temper. His phlegmatic lack of motivation and sanguine carefree attitude will cause him to forget appointments, be consistently late, and have a difficult time keeping his priorities straight. The "list" in his room is invaluable, and it is especially important not to "bail him out" of the sticky situations in which he finds himself as a result of his forgetfulness. If you drive him to school after forgotten assignments or books, he will learn to depend upon you instead of himself. A walk in the rain will be a good reminder of the importance of paying attention. If you make excuses for him, he will begin to make excuses for himself. If a few people become angry with him, and a project or class or church service is made less effective because of his undependability, it will be the best lesson he can learn. If he forgets to take out the garbage and he has to pay for the extra pickup out of his allowance, he will be less likely to forget again. If he forgets to come home to dinner on time, and the food is put away, his memory will improve. Be sure to explain the importance of this training in his future life, and that you are acting in his best interests. He must overcome this forgetfulness if he is to remain employed as an adult.

The answer to all the temperament weaknesses is, of course, a full commitment to the Lord. The only way for you to help your children accomplish this is by the best example you can possibly live, plus a lot of callouses on your knees!

3

"Home, Sweet Home"

What is a home? It is a place of refuge; a place where a person can rest and be safe; a seat of domestic life and interest.

Many homes are merely "houses." The song says, "There's no place like home," not "There's no place like a house." "Home" brings the connotation of warmth, laughter, the good smell of things baking in the oven, clean sheets, a family around a table with their heads bowed in prayer, a dog's friendly bark and wagging tail, a fire in the fireplace and a bowl of popcorn, games on a rainy day, the smell of a Christmas tree. But to many young adults, home is a place they are glad to leave with the determination theirs won't be like it. It is a showplace which is always utterly immaculate but not a place to bring your friends; or it is a cluttered, sticky, dirty place where the walls are lined with garbage bags. It's a place where you mustn't read a magazine unless you put it back in the rack in its proper position; or it's a place where you couldn't find a magazine to read if you wanted to because they're scattered all over the house in separate pieces. It's a place where one's bedroom is inspected daily and posters and all the memorabilia of growing up are not allowed; or it's a place where clean clothes are unheard of and matching socks call for a celebration! There is either "no playing on the grass and no snacking from the refrigerator" or there is no grass because it died for lack of care and water and the refrigerator is empty because Mom never gets around to grocery shopping. Both of these homes would discourage a young person from wanting one like it . . . either because it's a showplace with gleaming furniture and a model-home appearance, but never a source of comfort or relaxation or—because it's such a filthy mess—it's embarrassing to bring anyone home.

The "Hospital Clean" Home

If your home fits the first category . . . that of a shining, immaculate monster which takes all Dad's money and Mom's energy to keep up—but never seems to let kids breathe without that tight feeling that they might break something, spill something or move something—ask yourself "Why?" Are you really keeping this kind of house for your family? Or is it a source of pride to impress your friends and neighbors of your material wealth, good taste and organizational abilities? The "model home" may be lovely to look at but it is a horror in which to live. It is never a congregating place for young people. Granted, many parents are thankful for this. A group of high schoolers enjoying cokes and snacks in the kitchen or family room means things "out of place," crumbs on the furniture and scuff marks on the floor. But there are compensating factors. When young people are comfortable in your home, you will find communication to be open. Their response to you will be one of respect and love. You'll share their confidences and be asked for advice. Your relationship with them will become very precious to you and you'll wonder about the people who think teenagers are monsters. They'll even help you clean up if you ask them. Your time will be so much better spent molding a young life that will last for all eternity than scrubbing a house that will last only for 50 years or so.

The Mouldy Mansion

If your home fits the second category, you need to take a look at your priorities. What is taking the place of the homemaking you should be doing? Is it the TV soap operas or quiz shows? Is it committee work and "do-gooder" type activities? Is it coffee klatches with the neighbors? Or is it even church work . . . worthwhile and necessary . . . but undermining your home at this point. Whatever it is, you would do well to pray and ask God to reveal to you which of your time-consumers must be cut down. Certainly your husband can't appreciate this type of home, and you are training your children to either follow in your footsteps or take the opposite course and have the first type of home we described when they marry. Maybe you need to rise earlier in the morning, or maybe you never learned to organize your time and put "first things first." There are many books available in the library and in Christian bookstores which are written to help the housewife to do her chores more efficiently. If you can't find any of these, swallow your pride and consult an older friend or neighbor whose home seems to represent the type you would want, and ask her to help you to set up a schedule and to give you hints on easier ways to do things than those you have used in the past. Also pray that God will deal with your procrastination, slothfulness, lack of ambition or desire.

In either of these homes, where the children are discouraged from gathering, you will find that when they are grown and married, they will make excuses to avoid visiting you. They won't be dropping in to share their joys, disappointments or future plans. And later, when beloved grandchildren appear on the scene, they will be reserved toward you because they won't see you often enough to get to know you. When holidays roll around, you'll receive a short "duty visit" and then it will be, "Mom and Dad . . . I hope you won't mind, but we promised the in-laws we'd spend the day with them." And they will hurry out the door, leaving you to listen to the silence of your house . . . the place you created while they were growing up.

When In Rome . . .

For those of you who love having young people around, you don't have to sacrifice neatness or let your home be destroyed by a gang of wild teenagers. House rules need to be obeyed but they can be shared in a loving manner. For instance, the refrigerator is not community property. Inform your own children and their friends that they are welcome to a snack, but they must first check with you as to what is available to them. It isn't right for them to help themselves to the fruit you are counting on for lunches all week. And the breakfast orange juice needn't be gulped down as an after-school thirst-quencher. Have on store a supply of inexpensive snacks . . . canned fruit drinks, Kool-aid, lemonade, iced tea, the instant cocoa made with water for cold days, plenty of peanut butter, jelly and bread; cookies or cake or fruit in season. Insist they clean up after themselves. If you do it for them, they will begin to expect it of you and you will be teaching them that it is right to be thoughtless of others. Be good-natured about it as you call them to K.P. duty. They won't be offended and will be glad of the discipline.

If you have a pool table, ping-pong, swimming pool or other attraction which makes your home the preferred gathering-place for the gang, have a set of rules posted so there will be no misunderstanding as to their use. Insist they ask your permission before descending upon you and taking over their use, in case you have previously invited company, or for some other reason it is not convenient for them to be there. Your husband and you can draw up a sensible guideline for their use so that they may be enjoyed by your family to the fullest, and yet not exclude the children's friends. In the case of a pool, the best rule the Johnsons found was that those under junior high age must be accompanied by parents. This prevented them from having to "baby-sit" the gang when they swam, and also cut down on the visits because they had to take place at the parent's convenience. It also absolved them of responsibility in case of injury. Another rule they made was, "No using the pool unless adults are home to supervise" as the children got older. A pool table also needs adult guidance to prevent damage to the table or misuse of the cue sticks. Ping-pong is pretty safe and your only concern would probably be the number of young people who would show up at the same time.

Potluck With Pals

The Johnsons found that by making a once-a-week economical dinner and allowing their children to invite friends was a great way to get to know them and to win their confidences. Spaghetti, chili, pizza, tacos, barbecued hamburgers or hot dogs, are all kid-pleaser dinners, and easy to prepare and serve. They can be made inexpensively in large amounts and the leftovers can be frozen. This was usually done on a Friday night when the children were younger, but as they got into their teens, it was changed to a weeknight so as not to conflict with school activities. The children and their friends appreciated these times as they grew up, and when they had families of their own, many of them began this practice in their homes.

Your relationship with your children depends largely upon your acceptance of them as real people, the importance you place on your time together, and whether you are providing a real "home" for them. It's a risky business raising children today with so many outside influences to woo them away from Christian principles. Movies, TV, schools, magazines, and non-Christian friends tempt them to a degree that our generation finds hard to understand. A few years ago, the popular TV programs were characterizing good clean family life, such as "Ozzie and Harriett," "Leave It To Beaver," "Father Knows Best," etc. Now they are suggestive, with overtones of immorality, and rebellion on the part of the children. We need to build communication with our children while they are still young enough to spend some time in their homes. Depending upon the Lord as your best guide, and asking His guidance in making your home—"a place your children love to be"—is the answer.

4

Remember When a "Long Hair" Was a Classical Musician?

There have probably been more family disagreements over hair in the past decade than in any time in history. The Beatles started it, the beatniks of Haight-Asbury in San Francisco took over from them, and the hippies of the drug scene in current years wear it as their badge of defiance. Long hair came in with a "hassle" and is still a major source of irritation between fathers and sons, school officials and students, employers and employees and Armed Forces officers and recruits. If the style had been started by someone like Pat Boone or Billy Graham, there would have been no stigma attached to it. It also would undoubtedly never have caught on!

Fads are by and large a teenager's "thing" and most of them are harmless and pass quickly. The year Scott was a senior in high school the boys were wearing colored tee shirts with thermal underwear tops underneath them . . . in California, yet! In Lynn's class, it was long, straight hair done on the ironing board, if necessary, to get the kinks out. Three years later, kinks were "in" and everyone (male and female) looked like Little Orphan Annie.

However, with long hair on guys came the radicals. They marched, they hated and destroyed. Therefore, many of the nation's fathers associated longer hair with rebellion, lawlessness and drugs. Though Henry Snodgrass, the brainiest kid in school, still wore horn-rimmed glasses, carried a briefcase and got straight "A's" his father was certain he was going to the dogs when he asked to have his hair longer. The situation was understandable from the young boy's point of view . . . it was "cool" to have long hair. Yet when their parents saw on TV news the unwashed hippies shouting obscene words with their hair below their shoulders, they were appalled and disgusted . . . and rightly so! There seemed to be no common ground where parent and teen-age son could meet on this issue. The result was the "generation gap"!

The Hair Hassle

Jim Johnson was no exception to this rule. He wanted his sons to look presentable; yet, all three of them were beginning to "forget" to get hair-cuts, and for the two older boys, shaves were becoming more infrequent. They made excuses: "I got up too late to shave this morning!" or, "I'm out of razor blades," or "The barber shop was too crowded and I was in a hurry." The "hair hassle" got to be so frustrating that a family powwow was in order. After a time of prayer and discussion, it was decided that the boys could have their hair to the top of their shirt collars, and side-burns to the bottom of their ears. Mustaches would be permitted . . . beards would not. (Jim's reasoning on the beards . . . even short, trimmed ones, was mainly because of the complexion problem. It is more difficult to clean the face thoroughly when wearing a beard, and many young boys develop acne underneath their fuzz.) These rules were agreeable to everyone because the boys were apprehensive before the powwow that their dad would not give in to their desires at all. Jim realized that to insist on his own way completely would damage his relationship with his boys. Yet few businessmen would hire anyone whose appearance is offensive to others, even if their character is above reproach. The boys knew that when their father made a decision, he stuck to it until he was convicted otherwise, and they had to abide by it as long as they were living at home.

If hair is a hassle in your family, the first thing to do is examine your own motives. Is your son's appearance so bad that he is at odds with his family and teachers and unable to find employment? Or is the whole disagreement a result of your wounded pride in front of your short-haired business acquaintances? Is the long, past-the-shoulder length hair a badge of rebellion for your son, or is he a well-behaved boy, respectful to his elders, with a desire to be "in style" or "cool"? The Johnson boys had two very long-haired friends who were fine young men . . . planning to enter the ministry, constantly in the Word and involved at their church. Sometimes God chooses to deal in other, more important areas in our lives and leaves our appearances till later. Don't let length of hair become a wall between you and your son. Decide, with your mate, on a realistic compromise, then follow the Johnson's example. Have a meeting with the "long-hairs" of your family, beginning with your prayer for God's direction, and calmly discuss each side. Then give your decision and adhere to it until God leads you to change it. Your children will respect you more for upholding your standards than they will if you completely give in to their demands just to keep peace.

Since we are discussing boys in this chapter, we should mention that sometimes cleanliness is not one of their priorities. It was evident when Tommy first became interested in a girl in 8th grade . . . he went from as few showers as possible to two or three each day! The Johnsons insisted their children brush their teeth after each meal and before bedtime, and Lynn and Scott wore braces to correct minor bite problems. Skin care was another area of concern, and although Tom and Scott had drier skin and needed only thorough cleansing each night to maintain clear complexions, Mike and Lynn both required the aid of a dermatologist's treatment to keep their oily skin "zit-free." A bad complexion can be a source of insecurity and embarrassment to teenagers, and it is not necessary. One or two visits to a skin doctor and following his prescribed treatments are usually all that is required. He will normally recommend a fat-free diet, extra cleansing with an oil-free cleanser, and a mild antibiotic to clear up infections. The cost is relatively small compared to the benefits received.

None of the Johnson children had a weight problem, due partly to the well-balanced, nutritious meals prepared by their mother. Instead of rich desserts, there was fresh fruit or ice cream. Pies and cakes were reserved for weekends or company nights, and plenty of fresh vegetables and salads were available for dinner. Meats were lean and milk was low-fat. A good breakfast was a "must" and junk food such as potato chips, candy, pretzels, peanuts, etc., were not a daily fare. Nancy would often make popcorn (without butter) in the evenings because it is low in calories and serve it with iced tea or lemonade. If you have a youngster who is overweight, have your doctor check him to make sure it isn't a physical problem and if not, ask for a diet for him. Then see that he sticks to it. Set a good example by limiting your own snacks and offer the reward of new clothes or some special desire to be fulfilled when the ideal weight is reached. If the child has more than ten pounds to lose, you might want to do this in stages. After a certain number of pounds are lost, a new football or some hiking boots or whatever his particular interest would indicate. Provide an incentive, plenty of encouragement and understanding, and compliment him when he is losing but don't nag when he slips.

Marty Manners or Sidney Slob

One area sadly lacking in young men today is that of good manners. True, Women's Lib discourages the courtesies which men paid to women in years past, but there are still a number of Christian girls who would appreciate having doors opened for them, being helped in and out of cars, and having the offer of an arm while going up or down stairs. Sons need to be instructed to *always* call at the door for a girl, and to walk her to the door and see that she is safely in the house after a date. Table manners need to be taught at home, too . . . the Johnsons instructed their children in a loving way during family meals, but never in front of others. Good posture at the table is important . . . the chin-in-the-plate-shoveling-in-the-grub act noticeable in many teenagers was not allowed. Jim remembered telling his parents when he was a little boy, "Fingers were made before forks!" and having them answer, "But not *yours!*"

Share The Chores

Many boys are raised with no knowledge of housework at all and with the idea that it's beneath them and "women's work." In the Johnson home, where there were three boys and only one girl, household chores were distributed evenly, regardless of sex. Everyone helped to clear the table, and each child had two nights of loading the dishwasher. Schedules of chores were posted on a sheet on the kitchen bulletin board and each child was responsible for his own room and each had specific chores to do such as mowing the lawn, taking care of the pool, weeding, dusting and vacuuming. They were all shown how to run the washer and dryer in case something extra was needed, and each were taught the basics of cooking. Mike appreciated these instructions when he was grown and sharing a house with four other young men. Tommy's wife later told his mother what a help he was with the household chores when she was pregnant and when their son was born. Wives do become ill and a husband needs to know how to take over at these times. What better place to learn than in their own homes as they are growing up!

Fathers Are Fabulous!

As boys get older, they need the companionship of their fathers even more than when they are toddlers. Fathers need to develop hobbies with their sons and encourage them to participate together. Jim Johnson loved sports and his boys were sports fans, too. He taught them to play baseball, to fish, to play golf and tennis, to swim, and he was always at their Little League games and school activities unless there was some prior commitment which he could not postpone. He was interested in their problems and encouraged their talents and would work with them tirelessly. He would play "catcher" to their pitching, spend hours rebuilding a mini-bike motor or sanding a piece of furniture with them. Instead of repairing things for them as they matured, he explained how it was done and urged them to do it on their own. They learned to do household repairs that would prove invaluable to them in later years when they had their own homes, just by their understanding of the basic principles of electricity, plumbing and woodworking.

Though his musical training was nil, Jim was Scott's biggest fan, and always had time to listen to a new song he'd written or an arrangement he'd done on tape. Croquet, badminton and volleyball were games the whole family enjoyed and when winter came, they would gather around the kitchen table to play monopoly or hearts or work jigsaw puzzles. (These were done on pieces of plywood that could be moved to another location at mealtimes.) He taught his kids to play chess and carefully supervised their TV (which was much easier in those days when there was still censorship to keep trash and pornography out of our homes).

Helping with homework was a specialty of Jim's, just as a listening ear was right up Nancy's alley. A close communication was maintained between the Johnsons and their children's teachers. A special problem was a matter of prayer and there was no homework paper that was too difficult for God to solve.

The Birds and the Bees

The area where boys most differ from girls as they are entering their teens is that of sex. Girls rarely develop their sex drive as young as boys, and this is an area for dads to handle. A good book for parents to read on dealing with sex is *Sex Is A Parent Affair* by Liza Scanzoni. It is usually more difficult for mothers to communicate with their sons in this area just as it is for fathers to talk to their daughters about menstruation. It is important for fathers to impress upon their sons God's moral standards. The Book of Proverbs deals with this in a fantastic way, never becoming outdated. Boys need to be taught that fornication is wrong and that when a young man unites himself sexually to a woman, he becomes "one" with her (I Corinthians 6:16). The world's standards of sex are far removed from God's standards, but we will all be judged according to *His* standards. It is imperative that our children know exactly what they are! We will explore this subject more thoroughly in Chapter 6.

Why Work?

Jim Johnson was a great admirer of Paul, the Apostle. He was also insistent that his boys work. They would pray for God to open the doors for a job when each boy reached the age of 16 and could obtain a work permit. Then they would scan the newspapers, school and church bulletin boards and talk to friends and neighbors about any openings they knew to be available. The Johnson boys worked as busboys, gasoline-attendants, janitors and doing landscapers work while in high school. In college, each of them was provided with the perfect job by the Lord which would not conflict with their hours in school. Tom worked for a friend's father who owned a business. Each night for an hour and Saturday mornings he would vacuum, mop, wash windows and empty ashtrays and wastebaskets. He earned enough money to pay for his gas, spending and clothes. His parents paid for books and tuition for each of the children to encourage them to go on with their educations, and also room and board if the school was in another city. This would have to be adjusted as to family income . . . some simply cannot afford this and it would be up to the young person to earn a larger portion. Since the Lord had blessed the Johnsons financially, they tried to give their children a balance between help and responsibility. Mike worked as a caretaker in an electronics plant, doing the lawns and general "handyman" tasks afternoons and Saturdays. Scott trained as a school bus driver and drove morning and afternoon runs before and after his own classes. This was the best paying job of the three but was also the most time-consuming.

Unemployment Is Uncool

It is true that jobs are scarce, but God promises to supply all the needs of His children (Philippians 4:19) and He will never fail us. Fortunate is the Christian man who owns his own business because he can train his sons at a young age to help, and teach them to make worthwhile contributions. The Bible encourages everyone to work . . . in 2 Thessalonians 3:10 it says, *If anyone will not work, neither let him eat!* And Colossians 3:23 *Whatever you do, do your work heartily, as for the Lord rather than for men* (NASB). Jim taught his children to respect the positions of their superiors at work, even if they were unbelievers and they couldn't respect some of their opinions. Respect for authority is one of the most important lessons your sons will ever have to learn, and without it they will have great difficulty living as God intended. The Bible is very clear on this in Ephesians 6:5-6, Titus 2:9 and Colossians 3:22, among others.

The Johnsons cared deeply about their children's lives and stressed family prayer and open communication. They came to realize how few parents are concerned when they found themselves running a "second home" for countless friends of their own kids. They also observed that all through the years, it was the same group of parents who worked on the committees, attended the games and supported the functions. Jim and Nancy were obedient to God's command to *Train up a child in the way he should go: and when he is old, he will not depart from it* (Proverbs 22:6). Their commitment to Christ and desire to do God's will made them want to be the best parents possible to their children.

5

Department Store Dressing Rooms . . . or . . . Connie Claustrophobia

It is a rare mother of a teenaged daughter who can't identify with our title to this chapter. Nancy Johnson told friends that she was beginning to walk with her shoulders "squished in" because of the many hours she spent in cramped dressing rooms. She was convinced those tiny little "boxes" they call "fitting rooms" were designed by men who had never had to enter one! Picture yourself in a space about 2' x 3', with a dozen or so garments hanging on hooks on opposite walls, a mirror on one wall, a chair where you sit holding all your daughter's wearing apparel, her purse, her coat, your own purse, and several packages purchased at other stores, in 90 degree heat—while you dodge her elbows and knees as she gets in and out of blouses, sweaters, pants and dresses! Not exactly the ideal way to spend an afternoon! But, believe it or not, one to look back upon with a smile after she is married.

A "Fun" Mother

Nancy and Lynn were not only mother and daughter . . . they were good friends. Not in a "palsy-walsy" sort of way with Nancy following the fads and styles of Lynn's friends, but in a "sweet fellowship of Jesus" way where they could enjoy their shopping trips or going to lunch and long talks in the bathroom while Lynn set her hair in rollers and shared the truths God was teaching her. Nancy always dressed and acted like Lynn's mother, but a "fun" mother who was interested in all her boy problems and activities at school and church. They had real communication and there was nothing that Lynn felt she couldn't discuss with her mother.

Data for Raising a Daughter

When Nancy's neighbor asked her the secret of her relationship with her daughter, she was forced to stop and think about the factors which brought it about. She wrote them down on a sheet of paper, as follows:

1. Be consistent in prayer with your daughter
2. Be consistent in listening to her
3. Be consistent in discipline
4. Be consistent in your own walk with the Lord.

Nancy listed consistency in prayer as the first point. She took time to pray with each of her children, daily, throughout their lives at home. A short prayer before school in the morning, at bedtime except on date nights when she went to bed first, and the extra times which were perhaps the most meaningful . . . in the car on the way to a lesson or activity; at home over a snack after school; in their rooms when they were upset or frustrated; before studying for an examination; before or after a date; and even in dressing rooms on shopping trips (that God would choose the right clothes for Lynn). It isn't necessary to be in church or on your knees to pray. If Peter had had to wait to kneel when he called out his "Lord, help me" prayer as he was trying to walk on the water, he'd have drowned. You don't have to pray with your eyes closed, and you don't have to stop whatever it is you are doing. You can pray together while making a bed, or doing dishes, or driving in the car (make sure the driver keeps her eyes open!) or working in the yard. Nancy and Lynn often prayed while taking walks for exercise. This prayer time will strengthen your relationship with your daughter (or son) and give it a dimension you never dreamed possible.

Nancy's ready ear for her children's joys and problems made her their number one sounding board. Girls usually begin making a big thing out of boys at a very young age . . . (someone has said about playpen age through college). They may also have rather frustrating relationships with their girlfriends. There are jealousies, disappointments and minor scraps which are traumatic for them. Listen to their problems with the same attention you would give to a friend who came to you with a serious marital problem. Don't just dismiss them in an offhand manner with an "Oh, you'll grow out of it, dear." You will discourage further communication if you fail to take their problems seriously. The best solution, of course, is prayer. You will be giving the problem to God and at the same time teaching your daughter where her strength lies.

Be understanding of the puppy love affairs. Nancy could always recall her own youth and frustrating relationships with boys, and was able to be properly sympathetic to Lynn's disappointments.

Consistency in discipline is very important, and if you have practiced this while your daughter is young, it will probably not be a big problem during her teen years. However, if your daughter is disobedient and uncummunicative, you need to sit down together and discuss the fact that your relationship isn't what it should be. Ask her to forgive you for not being the kind of mother God intended, and tell her that from now on you intend to follow His way. If you have neglected her spiritual training, tell her so. If you have been too làx or too harsh with discipline, tell her that. Lack of discipline usually results in a demanding girl with no respect for your position as her mother. What she is really saying in her disobedience is "Prove to me that you really care by making me behave as I should!" You and your husband should discuss ways you can improve in the area of discipline, and when he makes the decision, back him up completely! Remember, God gave your children the kind of father He knew they would need, and even if you don't agree with your husband, you *must* agree with God!

It is difficult for a child to yield to discipline if she (or he) does not understand the principle of authority and submission. Each of us must learn to submit to those above us in authority. However, the higher the position, the more responsibility it carries with it. Children must submit to the authority of their parents, and mother must submit to father, but she also has the responsibility of a certain amount of the discipline of the youngsters. Dad, as the head of the house assumes the most authority, but he is responsible to God for his family. Since all authority is from God (Romans 12:1, 2) children must learn to respect their parents, teachers and government because of the position given the leaders by God, even if the person, himself, does not merit respect.

Consistency in your own walk with the Lord is necessary if you are to follow through on these first three points. Children learn more by what you do than what you say. If you are depending upon the Lord, totally committed to His will for your life, and experiencing the peace and joy of the abundant life, more often than not your children will want to follow in the same way. If you have an up and down spiritual walk—and one moment you are in the Word with your daughter and tuned in to her problems, and the next you are screaming, "Leave me alone!"—she will not be able to depend upon you and there will be a wall between you.

Don't Be Drastically Dressed

The most important thing you can give your

daughter next to faith in Christ, is self-confidence. Even attractive girls can be insecure and shy, and although it is not good to build your daughter's ego to the point where people find her offensive, she needs to know that she looks nice and is dressed appropriately. This is your responsibility as her mother. Dad can give his opinion, but you are the one who helps her shop. Modesty should be the key to a sharp Christian girl. Nancy had many talks with Lynn about the effect of a girl's manner of dress on a boy. Her brothers agreed with the fact that many girls dress to ''turn the boys on'' but that these weren't the kind of girls that they were proud to date. She was not allowed to wear skirts that were short enough to be revealing when she bent over or sat down, necklines which revealed her bosom, or pants of the low ''hip-hugger'' type that exposed a large area of stomach. Bikini bathing suits of the low cut type were a ''no-no'' and she wore shoes whenever she left the house. This was not only because of the safety factor, but because dirty, filthy feet are not attractive. The final inspector on matters of dress was Lynn's father. He viewed her clothes from a man's standpoint, and as the head of the home was responsible to God for the standards set for his family.

What if your daughter or son is an older teenager and does not dress according to your standards? You can only warn them of the dangers of immodesty, set a good example yourself, and pray for them. Don't underestimate the power of prayer . . . one small prayer is more influential than all the nagging in the world.

"My Mother Didn't Tell Me. . . ."

The mother who does not find time to teach her daughter how to cook, mend, clean, iron, wash and shop is doing her a very great injustice. It would be the same as taking her out to the middle of the ocean in a boat, throwing her overboard and saying, "I hope you enjoy learning to swim!" Nancy had to learn these things the hard way . . . *after* marriage! Her mother was a fastidious housekeeper and too impatient to take the time to instruct her in the proper way to do things. "It's easier to do it myself!" she would always say. Granted, it *is* easier than putting up with wrinkled beds, loose seams and dark clothes with lint all over them from the towels. However, marriage has enough adjustments without purposely adding that of a young wife who has not mastered a single household task and a husband who expects a clean house, decent meals and clothes in his drawer. The little extra time you take to teach your daughter these tasks will be more than worth it when you see the proud look on her new husband's face as she serves you a delicious dinner in her neat, well-decorated home.

Nancy encouraged Lynn to take some home economics courses both in high school and college as electives, where she learned additional skills and new ideas. Homemaking talent comes with practice, and that is why you can give your daughter the best training in the world right in your own home. Nancy observed that most of her neighbors who "hated housework and cooking" were those who had to struggle through learning it on their own and were unable to overcome the resentment of those early years of frustration.

The Working Gal

We stressed in the previous chapter that boys should be given the responsibility of a job as soon as they are old enough. This is important for girls, too. Babysitting is a good way to start, and there are usually plenty of jobs available for a good sitter. Be sure to stress the importance of their caring for someone else's children, and don't send your daughter out to sit for a young baby if she has had no experience caring for one. Lynn baby-sat in the neighborhood when she was 15 and her parents were nearby in case of emergency. Jim laughingly recalls the time she was sitting for three children a few doors away when the electricity went out. He immediately put on his coat to go to the house to help her find candles, etc., and as he started down the front walk, he met Lynn coming in, with all three children in tow in their pajamas and robes. She wasted no time getting them up and heading for the safety of her parent's home.

Jobs for Janes

There are many types of jobs available for older high school girls . . . helping with light housekeeping duties, clerking in stores, working in the McDonald's and Jack-in-the-Box type restaurants, part-time office jobs. The Johnsons supplied Lynn's basic clothes, but she bought her own "frills" or fad items. It taught her that money does not come bubbling out of a well in a never-ending supply, and she learned to stretch her budget. As she started college, she attended school in another town thirty miles away. There were no dormitories, so she and a girlfriend shared a small apartment. Her parents gave her a lump sum each month . . . enough to cover rent, utilities, telephone and food. The first couple of months it was slim-pickin's in the refrigerator the last week, and they ate plenty of soup for dinner. However, they soon learned to manage their grocery money and to budget a certain amount for each week. If they were especially careful and had some money left over, they went out to dinner as a treat. Lynn learned to manage her money so well that she was able to save enough to buy her mother an extra special birthday gift with it.

Your relationship with your daughter is one of the closest you'll ever experience with another human being on earth, next to that of your husband. It's up to you whether it will be a source of joy or disappointment. An investment of your time while she is growing up will produce rewards in later years that will bless you "exceedingly, abundantly"!

6

Dating: Delight or Disaster?

"If there were only a rule book and a standard procedure for teaching dating behavior, it would be a best seller overnight," Jim Johnson said to his wife. "How do we know when to let them start, who to let them go out with, what time to make them come home, and where we should or should not let them go?"

Jim's problem isn't unique. This has caused many a parent concern and has resulted in over-strictness in some and too much laxity in others. What *is* the happy medium in dating rules, and where should we "bend" and when should we "clamp down"?

Frosh Fun

One good source of guidance is your church youth director. He is usually "up" on all the latest activities and knows the hang-outs in town which may have changed with the years and are no longer permissible places for Christian teenagers to frequent. If you have a good youth group in your church, this, coupled with games and activities at school, is enough social life for a high school freshman. The Johnsons belonged to a large church with a deep concern for youth, and they had a good Sunday school class for high schoolers, as "afterglow" following evening church, which usually progressed to the nearest pie shop for snacks afterward, a midweek Bible study in each section of town, and a weekend activity such as roller or ice skating, bowling, miniature golf, or a get-together and hot dog roast at the church or someone's home. If your church doesn't have this available, how about you and your husband and a few other concerned couples starting one? It would be good to have some mature Christian college kids to lead the Bible studies and act as sponsors. Meet with your pastor about it, and if he does not agree that it is needed, maybe you should visit other churches to find out what's missing at yours!

That freshman year at high school is a difficult one for most youngsters, and group dating is the answer to being with the opposite sex without too much pressure. By the summer after the freshman year, your son or daughter should be mature enough to begin single dating. The Johnsons had a rule that they always met the boys Lynn was dating before she went out with them. They never set exact times for any of their youngsters to be home because they were aware that there may be delays in getting served in a restaurant and that time passes quickly when you're having fun, and it's easy to leave ten or fifteen minutes later than intended. They didn't want their children speeding and driving recklessly just to get home on the dot of midnight! They specified "around midnight" or "approximately eleven" (depending upon where they were going) and there was a reasonable leeway allowed. Mike was the only one who occasionally abused this privilege, but a few weekends spent at home deprived of any outside activities encouraged him to be more prompt.

Give 'Em To God

Probably the biggest fear Nancy Johnson had when her children started dating was that of automobile accidents. This was alleviated as she and Jim knelt by their bed and gave the children's dating life to the Lord and asked for their protection with the understanding that what they wanted ultimately for each of them was His perfect will. From then on, both she and Jim were able to go to bed while the children were still out and go to sleep immediately. This is a classic example of God fulfilling His promise in John 14:27: *Peace I leave with you; My peace I give to you; not as the world gives, do I give to you. Let not your heart be troubled, nor let it be fearful* (NASB).

Courtesy Is Cool

The Johnsons had a deep interest in every area of their children's lives, and their date-lives were no exception. They didn't just send them out on their first date with a hearty "Have a good time!" They gave them instruction on dating etiquette and behavior. The boys were briefed on opening car doors, offering an arm while descending stairs, walking on the outside next to the curb, giving the order to the waiter, and other gentlemanly courtesies. Much of this they had learned by their father's example, but Jim made a point of going over it with them again before they even began group-dating. (Group-dating is going together in a mixed group, but pairing up; many times it meant singling out that special one to be a partner in miniature golf but with the security of the company of the whole crowd. It takes the pressure off the boy or girl who is shy and finds it hard to make conversation with the opposite sex.)

Lynn was given the instruction of proper responses by her mother. "Don't jump out of the car before he has a chance to open the door. If he doesn't do this, remain in the car and say something funny like, Hey . . . you forgot me! and if he says, 'Open it yourself, you're not crippled' you have a pretty good idea of his personality . . . he's selfish! He isn't anxious to please you; he's only interested in his own convenience!" One important phase of dating behavior which most parents find embarrassing to discuss with their teenagers is that of the physical realm. Mothers may tell their daughters "Don't let him get fresh" and dads may say to their sons "Behave yourself!" but specific instruction is ignored. Nancy told Lynn later that after her own mother said not to let the boy get "fresh," she spent the whole evening wondering what it meant!

When the Johnson children reached high school age, their parents talked openly with each of them about God's moral standards and what He expects of Christians. They explained that our sexual drives are very strong, and that feeding them leads to problems of self-control. Jim impressed upon his sons the advantage of treating girls as sisters in the Lord and that if they didn't initiate petting sessions, almost certainly the girl won't. The general rule they followed was, "A good-night kiss is okay if you really care about the girl and you're not dating others, but limit it to one and don't park in the car expecting to be able to carry this limitation through." If more sons were trained by Godly fathers, there would be less experimenting with premarital relations in the high schools.

Early Warning System

Nancy gave Lynn clear guidance as to her behavior on a date. "You set the standards on your dates," her mother said, "and it's up to you to keep them as God wants. Most boys will go as far as you let them, and always remember that they will share everything you do in the locker room with the other guys! Be sweet and fun but don't be 'easy.' Don't allow a boy to kiss you until you are sure that he is 'special' and there is no one else you wish to date. Don't kiss everyone you go out with and don't kiss on the first date. And no more than a goodnight kiss. Remember that boys get excited and 'turned on' much more easily than girls, and if you kiss up a storm, you're encouraging him to want to fondle you with his hands, and this leads to heavy petting which can lead to intercourse before you realize what is happening. Keep yourself pure for your husband . . . you will be so glad you did! Fornication is a sin . . . it is listed in the Bible in many places!'' Nancy shared the Scriptures with Lynn in Acts 15:20, 1 Corinthians 6:18; 1 Thessalonians 4:3 just as Jim did with the boys. They also shared 1 Corinthians 6:16 that if you unite yourself sexually to someone, you become ''one'' with them.

Open communication between the Johnsons and their teenagers was the rule rather than the exception, because it began when they were first able to talk. But what if your children are already teenagers and there is no communication? We suggest you do the following:

1. Pray and ask God for wisdom and understanding, claiming the promise in James 1:5.
2. Meet with each of your children, individually, beginning with the oldest. You might say something like this: ''God has shown me (and your mother or father) that we have not been the parents we should be. We would like to begin now to change things in our relationship but we will need you to help us. We want to ask your forgiveness for not taking the time to listen to you, but we would like to pray with you

right now and ask God to bless our family with the ability to communicate with each other." Then pray out loud. If you've never done this before, you may feel uneasy. Just talk to God as you would to your own father or a special friend who cares about you and your family. If you don't get a positive reaction from the kids the first time, don't give it up and say "It's too late." Remember Luke 1:37, *With God, nothing is impossible!*

3. Begin spending time with each child alone each week. Make this a sharing time . . . not pushing them for responses, but sharing experiences from your own life or the lives of others which pertain to dating and sex. Share from the Scriptures and make it clear to the child that what you desire is God's best for him or her.

4. Uphold your teenagers in prayer daily . . . that God will reveal to them areas he wants changed and that they will feel more open to confide in you. Pray for a loving attitude as they begin to do this. You may hear some things that you aren't expecting that may upset or shock you. If you react in anger, they will stop confiding in you.

The Unhappy Ending

Growing up is a painful process, and there

will always be those times when your teenager gets "dropped" by Mr. or Miss Wonderful. Tears from girls (and sometimes even for boys) are not uncommon and anger, frustration and even deep depression may occur. The best "salve" for the wound is Scripture. The Psalms are excellent for any type of grief . . . and they really are grieved at this time. Don't "cut down" the person who ended the relationship. This will only add to their disappointment and put them on the defensive and you in a nasty position if they get back together! The reason they are so sad is that the person was so "fantastic"! A positive outlook is best . . . share some experience from your own past . . . how hurt you were when so-and-so broke up with you, but how wonderful God was to bring Dad (or Mom) in place of that other person who (it turned out) wouldn't have been right for you at all. Share how God has a special "one" for each of us, and *that* one has all the qualities to make us extremely happy. If this one that has gone his own way is not God's best, then think how wonderful God's best is going to be!

Encourage your teenager to give his date-life to the Lord, and to thank God for ending a relationship that wasn't His best. Realize that it may be only temporary . . . that they may get back together at a later date because the timing is not right at this point. But know that

God is in control and that this thing which hurts so much is "Father-filtered" and that God can take away the pain and fill the aching heart with Himself, *if* they are willing. When the right to have that other person is relinquished, God nearly always brings someone else along who is much more "cool" or "neat" or whatever the current word is for "the best." Above all, be loving, understanding and compassionate. It may seem unimportant to you, but to the hurt teenager, his whole world is falling apart!

Non-Christians: To Date or Not To Date

What about dating non-Christians? If your teenager has not accepted Christ, you've got a problem! Other Christians are not going to be inclined to date him, and furthermore, he would probably not be interested in them because of their high standards. Your only recourse is prayer and plenty of it!

But what of the Christian dating the non-Christian? The Bible says in 2 Corinthians 6:14 *Do not be bound together with unbelievers!* (NASB) Does this mean "no friendships with the unsaved"? The Johnsons felt that they could not, in good conscience, make it a rule in their family. We are told to go into all the world with the Gospel. If we huddle together in our "Christian cliques" how is the Gospel going to get out? So, non-Christian friends were allowed in the Johnson family . . . up to a point! If the unbelieving child was interested in attending church, going places with other Christian kids, and upholding the same standards, it was felt that they were seeking and open to Jesus Christ. However, if they were defensive toward Christianity, uninterested in the activities, and pushing the Christian young person to participate in their worldly "fun," the friendship was discouraged.

When it came to dating, the Johnsons took a different view. They felt that the desire to date a person begins with a physical attraction, coupled with wanting to get to know the person more intimately. This made the unbeliever "off limits." Their decision was based on an experience through which they learned the hard way that "evangelical dating" (dating an unbeliever with the ultimate goal being to win him to Christ) was not God's will as far as their family was concerned.

Tommy's Trauma

Tommy was in high school and began seeing a neighbor girl who was not a Christian. The families were acquainted and the Johnsons had been witnessing to them. Although not church attenders, they were very respectable people with high moral standards. Their daughter, Jill, was a lovely girl . . . a good student who did not drink or smoke or belong to the "party group" at school. They were both juniors in high school and far from marriageable age, and the Johnsons consented to Tommy dating her. Jill spent much time at the Johnson home and they witnessed to her often. She asked many questions about Christianity but was unresponsive to Tommy's invitations to church. She seemed to feel that since she was a "good" girl, helping others, cooperative at school and obedient to her parents, she really didn't need God running her life. As the relationship continued, the Johnsons were concerned but believed she would be converted in a matter of time. She made no objection to Tom attending church and occasionally she would consent to go to a youth-group function. But most of their time was taken up with games at school, picnics, movies and just family evenings at home. As they entered their senior year, the relationship was still going strong, and Jill was beginning to push Tom for a deeper commitment to her. An engagement ring for graduation? Marriage after two years of college? Tom began to be frustrated. He knew he could not marry a non-Christian, and his parents and his youth pastor affirmed this. Every sermon he heard, every guest speaker and everything he read seemed to dwell on this point. It was becoming clear to him that he must know in his heart that Jill had made a commitment to Jesus or break up with her. He convinced her that she should make an appointment with his youth pastor, alone, and felt that if she did accept the Lord it was God's stamp of approval on a future commitment.

Later, the young man told Tom that he had counseled with her and answered her questions for well over an hour, and led her right up to the point of praying with her to receive Christ, only to have her back down at the last moment! "I can't do it now," she said. "I'll do it later!" He told Tommy that it had been his experience that when someone rejects Christ in that way, it was either years before they became a Christian, or not at all! Tom had his answer: God was saying "No" to the relationship. With aching heart, he told Jill his decision, and even though she was hurt to the point where she dated no one else for months, she could not bring herself to accept Christ as her Savior. Fortunately, she was too honest to "fake it" just to get the guy she wanted. Tommy was hurt, too, but was able to give the problem to the Lord, who blessed his obedience by bringing him a beautiful Christian girl, whom he later married.

A Hard Lesson

The Johnsons learned a valuable lesson from this experience. It's a risky business for a Christian to date a non-Christian. The attraction could grow into a lasting relationship and the young person could either experience the hurt of breaking off or the worse tragedy of being unequally yoked in marriage with an unbeliever. They had begun by trying to be open-minded about "evangelical dating," but God convinced them it was too dangerous. As the Johnson children observed their friends who dated unbelievers get pulled away from Christian activities and friends, they could see that it would make growing in Christ most difficult. Tom later admitted that his walk with the Lord had suffered while he was dating Jill steadily. He lacked fellowship with his Christian friends and missed many Bible studies, meetings and functions with his youth group. This resulted in his personal prayer life and study of the Word becoming slipshod. Non-Christians look at situations from a worldly standpoint instead of from God's view and tend to encourage those Christians with whom they are closely associated to do the same.

This has to be an individual decision for each family, but God showed the Johnsons clearly which course they should take with their own children. If you are confused or undecided in this issue, ask God to show you clearly what you should do. Remember James 1:5, *If any man lack wisdom, let him ask . . .*

Don't Spill the Beans

One thing for parents to remember when teenagers begin sharing is to keep their confidences. Nothing will disappoint them so much as to hear from a neighbor or friend that you have shared their problem. Confide in your husband (or wife) only, and possibly in a loving Christian grandparent, but *that's all!* If you betray their confidence, you betray their trust, and your communication will go down the drain!

7

'Fessin' Up

In the Arkansas hills, when someone gets on the wrong track, it's up to a good friend to "fess him up." That is, he discusses with him, in a loving way, where he believes him to be heading in the wrong direction. This could have a good spiritual application, too. In the Bible, we are told to bear one another's burdens, and to help our brother who is in sin, and to "take the log out of our own eye" and forgive as our Father in Heaven forgives us. All this involves inter-communication with each other.

The Runaway

For instance, when Mike Johnson was a junior in high school, he was at his most rebellious state. He was constantly cutting school; when he was grounded he crawled out his bedroom window after his parents were asleep and went out with his friends; his grades were slipping badly and he was often at odds with his parents and brothers and sister. Things finally came to the point where he felt the only thing to do was run away. He left for school one morning and didn't return home for three days. His parents were deeply concerned, but knew from questioning his friends that he had run away and was at the home of two boys they knew whose parents worked swing shift. Since they knew he had shelter and food, Jim and Nancy decided to just pray and wait it out. They went about their activities (outwardly) as usual, and made no attempt to contact Mike.

Meanwhile, anxious to see what effect his running away had on his family, Mike was sneaking near to his home and watching them each day. Hiding behind trees, bushes and fences, he observed his home and saw that life was "as usual" and that they were coming and going and sleeping and eating. (Sometimes those food smells were enough to make him give up and return.) Since the parents where he was staying were at work when the boys came home from school, and asleep when they got up in the morning, there were no warm breakfasts with bacon and eggs, and no luscious dinners with meat and salad and fresh vegetables. Peanut butter and jelly was the standard fare, and it was beginning to get pretty monotonous. He had not thought to bring extra clothes and had been wearing the same ones for three days. He had run out of money, and running away had lost its sense of glamor and excitement. He missed his bed, his room and, he had to admit, his family!

The Repentance

Afraid of the consequences of his venture, Mike decided that instead of going straight home, he would seek the counsel of his youth pastor, who was also his neighbor. The evening of the third day, he appeared at Ron's door and asked him if he would go with him to talk with his parents. Ron knew the situation, but questioned him at length to determine whether he was sincerely repentant. When he found he was, he accompanied him to his home. Jim and Nancy welcomed Mike home, and the family and the youth pastor sat down to pray together. Mike began to confess his wrong acts, and Jim and Nancy admitted that they had not been right in their relationship with him either. They had been too lenient about following through on punishment, had not supervised his selection of friends carefully enough, and had not spent enough time with him individually. Together, they prayed for a fresh start, open communication and the Lord's leading. Everyone "fessed up" and determined, with God's help, to do better.

Mike realized that there were friendships he was going to have to terminate. His parents realized that they had to stop expecting him to be more like Tommy. He was an individual and they needed to treat him as one. Mike's experiences with his friends and their lifestyles while he was living those few days away from home, proved to him that their bragging about their independence was a coverup for their insecurities. He had found out that the grass always *seems* greener on the other side of the street. Parents who were always gone, no rules as to dating or friends, and freedom to do as they pleased was really a kind of bondage. No punishment for doing bad also meant no rewards for doing good. There was no encouragement, no interest and no communication in those homes. Teenagers "did their own thing" while parents did theirs. It all boiled down to the fact that "no one cared." Mike found it depressing and frustrating, and realized how fortunate he was to have been born into a Christian family! All the mischief those other boys got into was merely a bid for attention from their parents.

The Requirement

However, Mike did not change overnight. Although he stopped seeing those boys who encouraged him to leave home, it was difficult for him to do a complete "about face" in his life style. It was spring and the surf was "up" and it was a great temptation to cut school and go to the beach, 30 minutes away over the mountains. Jim and Nancy prayed for God to give them wisdom and guidance in dealing with Mike, and God not only responded, He gave Mike a terrific sunburn every time he skipped school so his parents would know with one glance where he had been!

It required much time and effort on the Johnson's part to keep close tabs on Mike. He was 16 and many of his friends had cars, but with the Lord's help, nearly every time he was someplace he shouldn't have been, someone would see him and happen to mention it to his mother or father. (Usually in complete innocence.) This seeming inability to keep from getting caught was a good incentive for Mike to stay on the straight and narrow path. By the time his senior year rolled around, he had gotten into the habit of doing what was expected of him most of the time and had also become part of an entirely different crowd of boys. Most of them were from his church, and though not the most spiritual of the church's teenagers, they were from Christian families whose standards were the same as the Johnsons and none of them had ever been in any serious trouble.

Why Rebellion?

What was at the bottom of Mike's rebellion? Jim and Nancy Johnson realized that they needed to discipline him more, but they didn't understand why he had the tendency to be mischievous and was harder to deal with from the time he was very young. Their youth pastor gave them a clue. Mike's position in the family had much to do with it. He was the second son. His older brother was a quiet, talented, athletic student who seldom got into trouble. With his good looks and sense of humor, he was very popular with both boys and girls, and was obedient to and had good communication with his parents. Jim was interested in athletics, which automatically gave him and Tom a good rapport. He spent time with Mike, too, but his heart was not in racing cars or surfing. Mike's interest not being in sports as a participant, caused him to be unable to make the teams as anything more than a bench-warmer, for the most part, and he felt this disappointed his dad. Teachers tended to compare him with his brother in class and this added to the problem. While none of these points in itself is enough to make a rebellious son—put together with the personality of Mike—that was the result. Mike seemed to deliberately choose non-Christian friends, and the youth pastor told the Johnsons that this is always a danger signal. As parents, we need to watch for these "red lights" of warning in our children's lives. The choice of radical friends, a tendency to dress in a "hippie" fashion rather than like the Christian kids, problems at school, negative responses to parent's suggestions, and a bad attitude all spell t-r-o-u-b-l-e and need to be dealt with immediately. The pastor pointed out that when you notice that your car isn't running right, you don't jump out and hit it with a board or kick it. You take it to a mechanic and have it checked before it becomes a major problem. We should treat our children the same way; when they are not "running right" or responding as they should we need to sit down, pray with them, and try to discern their problems. If they are uncommunicative, then make an appointment for them to talk with their youth pastor, Young Life or Campus

Life leader or a mature Christian friend. Children are complex beings, and as they enter their teens, their complexity increases. Parents must be "on their toes" to prevent serious problems, so watch for these signs of potential danger.

8

Our Church Family

"You can worship God and be a Christian without going to church!" This is probably the standard comment of every person who has not met the Lord personally or does not understand the necessity of Christian fellowship to the believer. A Christian without a church is like an ember that flicks out of the fireplace onto the hearth, away from the other coals. Its flame eventually goes out!

Jim and Nancy Johnson were deeply involved in their church and rarely missed a Sunday . . . not because there was a rule that they had to be there . . . but because they loved the fellowship and the warmth of the Holy Spirit in the worship services. If they went to the mountains or the ocean for the weekend, they came home early for Sunday evening church services. If they were on vacation, they visited other churches wherever they happened to be. If they were camping, they attended services in the State Parks. Church was important to them, and their children were well aware of this from as far back as they could remember.

The Christian "Family of God"

"Why *can't* you worship God on your own, without getting up early on Sunday morning?" asked Jim's neighbor. "You can, occasionally," replied Jim, "but your Christian life would suffer without the teaching of the Bible by qualified persons, and you would be disobeying God's command to 'forsake not the assembling together of yourselves' (Hebrews 10:25). Besides, if you don't develop Christian friends, your tendency will be to look at every problem from the standpoint of the unbeliever. For instance, if your child is having a problem with a teacher, the advice of the unbeliever would probably be to go to the teacher and complain, and if that doesn't get results, see the principal, and if there is still no improvement, take it up with the school board! The Christian, on the other hand, would pray with you about the problem, and advise you to pray with your child about his own attitude and for God to work in the teacher's life. Within a short time, the situation would undoubtedly begin to change for the better, and the child would learn a valuable lesson of the power of prayer and also how to get along with others.''

"The Bible Tells Me So"

It is said that if we are not growing in our Christian lives, we are going backwards. And it would be very difficult to mature in our faith without the help of the church, Bible study and the other advantages the church offers such as special speakers, fellowship with the Body of Christ and training for out children. Parents need to set the example for their youngsters and if you drop them off at church, they're going to realize that it isn't very important in your life. As they grow older, they may rebel against going because you don't go!

What if you are a regular attender and your teenagers are rebelling against the church? The Johnsons insisted that as long as their children were living in their home, church attendance was mandatory. They pointed out the Scripture in Hebrews 10:25 and explained that they, in good conscience, must obey God. Proverbs 22:6 says *Train up a child in the way he should go: and when he is old, he will not depart from it.* This is a promise, and the Johnsons had claimed it. Therefore, they had to fulfill the condition which was the first part of the verse. If their children were ill and needed medicine, they would force them to take it. If they said they didn't like school, they still had to attend. And church is as necessary to a child's life as medicine or school. Hopefully, it will be more palatable than either one.

Is Your Church Still Breathing?

It is well to determine the cause of the unwillingness of your child to attend church. Is there a good youth group? Is there a youth pastor? Do they preach the Bible? Are they too legalistic or too liberal? Is it a tiny church with very few young people? Are you rather bored with the services but attend out of habit because your conscience bothers you if you are absent? Is your church alive and growing, or do you have about the same number of members as last year? If you answered "no" to any of the first three questions and "yes" to any of the next three, and your church isn't growing to any appreciable degree, maybe it would be well to visit other churches.

Jim Johnson's neighbor, Stan, belonged to a small church in their area. "Why do you drive five miles to that huge church where you can't possibly know everyone?" he asked Jim one day when they were out in the yard.

"Well, I realize that it is farther to drive and that I don't know everyone," replied Jim. "But I know in my heart that wherever the name of Christ is lifted up, and the Bible is preached regularly, God is blessing. And when He blesses, how can a church remain small? The Spirit of the Lord is so evident in our church that people immediately respond to the warmth and friendliness there, and it doesn't *seem* big. The early Church was *huge* and they had sweet fellowship together, so it's entirely normal for churches to grow.

"Well, that may be so," replied Stan, "but don't your kids get lost in the shuffle?"

"Our kids are so well ministered to that they can hardly wait for Sunday School classes and activities. They divide the large classes into small groups with each 8-10 kids having their own individual teacher. There is always something going on, and one of the biggest advantages of a large church is the extensive program they are able to provide for youth."

Stan looked thoughtful. "You know, we *have* been having a hard time getting our kids to church, and there are only about a dozen high schoolers who go there. They've been asking us to visit your church ever since they attended that special musical program with your kids a couple of months ago. Maybe we should give it a try.''

Don't Let the Devil Make You Do It

One of Satan's most successful tricks is to get Christians so involved in a dead church that they feel obligated to stay and ''help.'' They hope to be able to change things and influence their pastor to be more Biblically grounded. Don't be fooled by this trick of the enemy. You will seldom change anything; you will probably cause dissention. If Satan can get you to stay in a dead church long enough, your children will either have grown up without the benefit of Bible teaching and Scriptural principals or they will be turned off to Christianity by the legalistic rules and ''no-no'' list of your church.

Dead churches are usually either liberal, with a social gospel or works and a reluctance to believe the Bible, or they are legalistic, with a long list of ''don'ts'' that are unscriptural. A good church is as important to your family's welfare as a good home. Don't stick with a dead one because you have friends there or you hate to leave them in a bind! Go where the Gospel of Jesus Christ is preached and the

Word of God is opened at each service. Go where there is a good youth ministry and activities for your teenagers and children of all ages. Go where you are exposed to good speakers and seminars and prayer conferences. Go where they participate in a good Christian camping program. Many young people meet Christ at camp, or make a recommitment of their faith. There are fine Christian camps all over the country, and if your church does not encourage one, find out why!

Christian Camps Are Colossal!

Camp played an important part in the lives of the Johnson children. They all attended camps each summer, and Lynn and Scott both counseled when they were out of high school. Lynn was the most involved, serving on full-time staff for two summers at a Christian conference ground. Their camp experiences were times of concentrated learning from the Scriptures and the application of Truth. As adults, they looked back on these times as periods of great growth in their Christian lives. They made some lifetime friendships at camp, and saw many non-Christian friends converted and set on the path of full-time service to the Lord.

Church, to the Johnsons, was like a weekly transfusion. It provided strength to get from one week to the next. It encouraged their personal study and devotions, it provided outreach to unbelieving friends, it fed them new truths to apply in their daily lives, and gave them areas of service which helped them to grow spiritually.

9

Freedom In The Lord

"Why do my parents try to make me fit into some kind of mold? Why can't they just let me be myself?" lamented Dan, one of Tommy's friends. "My dad is a doctor, so he thinks I should be a doctor, too! I can't stand the smell of hospitals and the sight of blood makes me sick! I dig working outside and I'd like to be a landscape gardener or a farmer. Making things grow really turns me on, but every time I mention it to him he has a fit! 'No son of mine is going to work out in the dirt!' he says. If I don't agree with him on every single thing, *I'm* the one who's wrong!''

Be Like Me!

Tommy's father overheard their conversation and later said to Nancy, ''That was a good lesson for me to learn! I've got to quit trying to push Mike into sports when he just doesn't have the interest Tom does. I also need to give the Lord my dreams of one of the boys taking over my business. Tom doesn't like selling and wants to be a dentist; Mike would make a good salesman, but he would rather do carpentry work or some kind of building; Scott's big interest is music and he has plans to go into the ministry. Dan is right . . . we fathers often try to force our own desires on our sons.''

''Well, mothers are no exception,'' Nancy answered. ''We want out daughters to be cheerleaders and play the piano and be popular with the boys and marry someone *we* think is good looking and is well able to provide for them! When Lori down the street married that homely fellow who worked at the gas station, we were all disappointed. But now he owns his own garage and is a deacon at the church and has gotten better looking every year. The handsome athlete she was going with has been divorced twice! We can't see the future, but God can and He knows what's best for our kids!''

God's Love

God loves us unconditionally. He doesn't love us more if we perform better, pray more spiritually, study our Bibles more faithfully, or go into full-time Christian service. He is pleased with us, but He loves us all the time, all the same, just because we have Jesus in our hearts! We have trusted in His Son and this is how we become part of His family. He loves the newspaperman on the street corner who has trusted Christ as much as he loves Billy Graham, who leads thousands to Him every year! Why can't we love our children in the same way God loves us? Why can't we give them the freedom to be what they want to be? Possibly it is a matter of pride . . . *our* pride. We want our kids to be admired by others and to be what the world calls ''successful.'' Many parents discourage their children from going into the ministry or the mission field because they feel they won't be as ''successful'' as their friends who are going to be doctors, lawyers or businessmen.

Pray For God's Way

The most effective way we can guide our

children is through prayer. We can offer them suggestions as to their future, and we can help them to go to college, but we can't force them into a mold! A child who is weak and has a strong parent and is forced into the kind of work the parent wishes for him will be a miserable, frustrated, unhappy adult. Though he may be obedient to his parent, he could have feelings of bitterness toward him, and those bitter feelings may produce guilt. An overload of guilt can lead to a nervous breakdown, and the parent will wonder, "Where did I go wrong?"

We can pray for the Lord's will in the lives of our children and believe that He will answer. It may not turn out exactly as we expected but remember Isaiah 55:8 . . . God's ways are not our ways; neither are His thoughts our thoughts. His ways are so much more perfect than ours and so much better for our children that there's no comparison. He loves them so much more than we do—with a completely unselfish love. We can't equal that.

Dessert Devotions

Is there anything else we can do to guide our children into the right choices? God left us a rule book . . . the Bible. And in this Bible is the best instruction for raising children that was ever written: the Book of Proverbs! We hear a lot about family devotions, and it calls to mind a little altar with candles on each end, a Bible in the middle, and Father kneeling with his back to his family praying, while the others sit in a circle with their heads bowed. Very spiritual looking, but we've never yet met anyone who was able to get a 4-year-old, an 8-year-old and a teenager together at the same time each evening, have them all be quiet, keep the telephone from ringing and motivate them so that they were anxious to gather at this altar each night. A family "altar" is much more than that . . . it is a family worshipping together, praying together and reading together.

The Johnsons had their "family altar" at the dinner table each night, after the dishes were cleared. Jim Johnson had the Living Bible on the window sill next to the table. Each night, corresponding to the date on the calendar, he would read a chapter of Proverbs. Since there are 31 chapters, it works out perfectly. Occasionally it would not be convenient for everyone to be there or someone would have to leave early, but those who were there continued the practice. A good thing to remember about family devotions is not to be legalistic. Jim would read one verse, and then they would discuss it . . . each member of the family giving their opinion as they felt led.

Sometimes they would only get 5 or 6 verses read and discussed in 15-30 minutes, so the next time through that chapter (on the corresponding date of the next month) they would take up where they had left off. After they had been through Proverbs several times, they went to other books in the Bible. The whole family learned from this and later when they were all married, they continued these "dessert devotions" in their homes.

Through Proverbs in particular, the Johnson children learned why their parents disciplined them and why a rod was used. They learned why they should follow their parents' advice in moral matters. They learned that they should choose their friends wisely and that anger is a sin. The wealth of Truth in this book is never-ending and each time a chapter was read, new wisdom was gained from it.

This time in the Scriptures helped the children in their communication with their parents, because they were able to understand why their parents felt as they did about certain issues. At the prayer time at the end of the devotion, they found they could share things about which they normally would not be open. These "dessert devotions" built trust between parents and teenagers and Jim and Nancy learned to expect the best of their young people rather than suspecting the worst. Many of their friends were extremely suspicious of their teenagers, and these kids complained to the Johnsons that their parents accused them of things they hadn't even *thought* of doing. Suspicious attitudes create sneaky kids. We need to accept our children and their acts at face value until they are proved differently.

Most young people will respond in a positive way to their parents' trust. If you pray for God's wisdom in dealing with your children, you won't need to worry about trusting them; He will guide you.

10

When Trouble Comes

The Bible says if you train up a child in the right way, when he's old he will not depart from it. But what about the in-between years? If you train him right, is there any possibility that he might depart from the way *before* he is old? Do Christian kids get involved with drugs or have illegitimate babies or get into trouble with the police?

When It Hits Home

Jim and Nancy never thought this could happen when their children were small, but as they grew up they saw the heartbreak of Christian friends as these tragedies touched them. And suddenly they found that they, too, were experiencing trials with their second son, Mike. Through the counsel of a Christian coach at the high school, during his junior year, they searched Mike's room and found drug paraphenalia. He admitted experimenting but said he has stopped because he was beginning to experience "heart palpitations." They immediately took him to a good internist and had him take a complete physical. This kind doctor was very thorough . . . both in his examination and his advice to Mike. He pronounced him in perfect health and then proceeded to tell him how fortunate he was that he had not suffered permanent heart damage. He explained what "uppers" do to the metabolism and the vital organs of the body. Then he cited case histories of boys he had treated who did not fare so well. By the time Mike was through with the examination, he was mortally afraid to use drugs again. As an adult, he still spoke of how that doctor had frightened him, and how glad he was that his parents made sure someone who *knew* firsthand told him of the dangers of the drugs to the body.

Watch For Symptoms

Before it happened in their own family, Jim and Nancy could not understand how teenagers could experiment with drugs without their parents' knowledge if the mother was home all the time. They felt that if the father spent time with his children, knew their friends, kept strict rules and they were Christians, how could they *help* but know that their children were involved in something so serious? After their own experience, they found it to be common in many cases. When the coach came to visit them, he told them the symptoms to watch for in drug use. "If they are using marijuana, you will notice a sudden decline in their grades and interest in school. They will seldom follow through on anything they set out to do, and although they will make many plans, they will usually drop them. If they are in college, they may start out taking 16 units and end up with 4. Bloodshot eyes are also a physical symptom, as is stuttering."

The Methedrine or "speed" symptoms are hyperactivity. They may talk a great deal, lose their appetite and lose weight, but be constantly "on the go." Mike's experience with this drug was difficult to detect because he had always been a constant talker, had never had a big appetite and was of a more nervous disposition. His parents thought his more slender

---

appearance was due to his spurt of growth in height. Since he took pills by mouth, there was no sign of tracks on his arms as in many hard drug users. His clothes smelled of marijuana, but it was not noticeable to his mother when she put clean shirts in his closet because she had never (to her knowledge) smelled it and didn't know what it was. He kept his pills and joint-clips in his suit coat pocket which he wore to church, because his mother seldom had it cleaned, since he only wore it for an hour or two once a week; so God's providential hand was in his father going through that coat pocket.

Downers Are A Drag

The symptoms of "downers" are extreme lethargy, slurring of speech and slow movement of the body. This would be easier to detect. . .particularly in a child like Mike. They also experience a personality change with these drugs, and can become angry at the slightest provocation. If they drive a car, they often have accidents. . .particularly hitting parked cars as they experience a loss of coordination. Parents can call the Drug Abuse Center in their town and ask for pamphlets to be sent to them regarding symptoms, how to deal with the child on drugs and cures.

Bear One Another's Burdens

Their experience with Mike and Jim made Nancy much more compassionate toward others with problem children. When a Christian neighbor's daughter became pregnant, Nancy was the one who defended the parents and put a stop to the gossip. She prayed with the neighbor all through the long months of the daughter's pregnancy and when the baby was placed in an adoption agency immediately at birth, she was their strength. A loving, unjudgmental attitude helped the young girl through her ordeal and drew her closer to the Lord. She realized that her high school boyfriend was not ready for marriage and was also not ready to make a commitment to the Lord. Her parents' advice to put the baby up for adoption and take night courses in order to graduate from high school was followed, and even as an adult in later years, she never regretted her decision. She married a fine Christian man with whom she was completely honest about her past. This heartbreaking experience drew the whole family closer to the Lord, and they learned of His tender care for them. The young girl was extremely repentant and confessed her sin to God and to her family and friends, but, unfortunately, she still had to bear the burden of having the child. Our sins are always forgiven, but we still have to suffer the consequences.

Take Time

What about the incorrigible child . . . the one who becomes completely unmanageable? How can this be handled? The Johnsons never had this problem because Jim was a firm disciplinarian. Although Mike got into trouble, he never "talked back" to his father or openly refused to be obedient. He was always repentant when caught, and went through a period of unusually good behavior after that. His problem was a weak will and an inclination to slip back into his old ways after a time.

Jim and Nancy's neighbors, however, experienced a complete rebellion in their 16-year-old son. Bob, the father of the family, was a phlegmatic . . .easy going, with the tendency to "put off" discipline. In fact, there were times when he ignored it altogether and left it to his nervous, excitable wife. Her way was not any better . . . she was a "screamer" but seldom followed through on punishment. They simply could not cope with this son and gave up trying. He was failing in every area of his life . . . in school he had only enough credits to qualify as a freshman, although he was in his third year. He had had many traffic tickets and finally had his license revoked. He was taking hard drugs and was involved in petty theft and finally in grand larceny, though he was not caught. Still, his father refused to "get tough" with him. . .he did not believe in the rod of correction for any of his children, and this was the basis of the problem. Fortunately, his oldest son was a well-behaved phlegmatic and didn't need much discipline. The youngest boy, however, was beginning to follow in his brother's footsteps when Bob appeared at Jim Johnson's door asking for advice. Jim shared with him the Bible verses which instruct parents to use the rod (Proverbs 22:15, 23:13, 14) and others in Proverbs which encourage the father to discipline. They prayed together and Bob went home determined to set things straight with the Lord and with his family.

Always Follow Through

He got the whole family together in the living room and confessed that he had been wrong in not assuming his entire responsibility as a father. He had been lacking in the area of discipline and things would now be handled according to the Scripture. The oldest and youngest sons agreed, and prayed with their father and mother, but the middle one . . . the rebel . . . simply got up and left the room. His father talked with him later and told him that if his ways did not change, he would call the police and have him placed in Juvenile Hall. Not believing his father, the young man went to his room and was later overheard talking on the telephone to someone about some drugs he was planning to sell. His father immediately called the police, told them the entire story and instructed them to come and get his son. It was the hardest thing he ever had done, he said later, but one of the wisest.

After spending four days in Juvenile Hall, with the threat of being sent to a foster home, the young man was willing to do anything to remain with his family. His attitudes began to change after that, and he respected his father for following through on his word. He eventually committed his life to the Lord and turned from his wicked ways. There were still hard times, but he knew that his father would do as he said, and would take the time to be aware of his activities and be interested in what he was doing and who his friends were. When Bob began following God's instructions for child discipline, his family problems straightened out.

11

What About College?

There was a time when nearly every parent felt college was imperative to their children's future. Trade school or apprenticeship was thought to be only for those with less intelligence than normal, and being a doctor or lawyer was the "ultimate" goal! As thousands of young people graduated from college with teaching degrees and were unable to obtain employment, and with premed degrees and were unable to get into a medical school, the trend toward higher education began to change. Parents and counselors alike began to take a different view.

God's Best

The Christian parent has an obligation to encourage his child to seek God's best for him. In some cases, college isn't "God's best" and many young people graduating from high school are simply not ready for the pressures of a university. Many go on to junior college to get their educational feet wet, and find after a year or two there that they feel led to a certain field which requires more education, or that they would rather be in a trade or follow a different line of employment. The important aspect here is that the young person be excited and happy about his chosen field, and that he feels the contentment that comes from following God's plan for his life.

Different Strokes For Different Folks

Tommy Johnson wanted to be dentist from the time he was a little kid, and immediately started in a large university with a good dental school upon graduation. He enjoyed studying and the difficult science courses were interesting to him. Mike, after a year at a junior college, wanted to work for awhile and save money to travel. He worked for a year, saved enough to buy a van, and with another friend drove around the entire United States. He took the southern route from California to Florida, up the East Coast to the New England States, and went across the northern part of the country to the state of Washington and back to California. He called his parents at least twice a week, informing them of his whereabouts and his itinerary for the next few days. He and his boyfriend camped in State Parks (it was summertime) and stayed with friends or relatives whenever possible. The entire trip took about two months.

When he returned home, he still had enough money for a short trip to Hawaii to visit friends. With this travelling out of his system, he was ready to go back to school upon his return home from Hawaii. He got a part-time job in construction, building homes, and went back to the junior college for his second year. Through the construction job, he realized he loved building and began doing remodelling work to supplement his income. Working with a man who was very accomplished, he learned everything he could from him. At the end of his second year in college, he realized that he wanted to make building his life's work, and took a job with a large company as an apprentice carpenter. 'Upon completing his training, he moved to a resort community in the mountains and began his own business building and remodelling cabins. Higher education was not for Mike, but he was very content in his work and was able to support himself, and later his family, live where he pleased, pursue his skiing in the winter, and be involved in his church.

Scott's Tune

Scott, musical from his toddler days, had no problem deciding upon his life's work. He knew it had to be in the field of music . . . he just wasn't sure where. After high school, he followed his sister's footsteps and enrolled at a Bible college. After two years of study there, he transferred to a university where he obtained a degree in music. Combined with working in his own church, he was well qualified to follow his heart's desire as a music minister.

The Lord's Leading For Lynn

Lynn had the desire to go on to college her first year in high school and it continued through graduation. She attended a small college in a town a short distance from her home. After a semester in a secular college, she realized that she was "out of place" among the non-Christians and the marijuana smoking, loose-moralled girls with whom she was surrounded. Although her roommate was a Christian with the same standards as Lynn, she was engaged to a young man away in the service and had no desire for any social life. Lynn didn't wish to date non-Christian boys and there were very few Christians on the campus. She was also not happy with her courses or the teachers, who often "put her down" for her beliefs. The required reading included books that were bordering on the pornographic . . .best-selling novels with detailed sex passages, and her art classes featured live, nude models who walked around the classrooms and conversed with the students in the "altogether." At the end of the semester, she transferred to a Bible college, where she happily pursued a two-year counselling degree.

Lynn spent her summers working at a Christian camp and her college days teaching Sunday School in her church and singing in the choir. She met a young man in the bass section who was studying for the ministry, and fulfilled her life-long dream of being a wife. She was a big help to him in his studies after they were married, with her background at the Bible college. She had taken secretarial courses in high school and was able to find employment in a pediatrician's office. Then she learned information on caring for sick children which prepared her for the rearing of the five little ones she and her husband desired.

Practice Advice

Lynn was not particularly interested in taking the typing and business courses in high school as electives that her parents suggested. They counseled her as to the importance of a girl being able to support herself since most women need to work before marriage, some after—until the babies come—and some still later if they are widowed. She was happy to have followed their advice as her salary as a secretary-receptionist helped to make it possible for her husband to stay in school. With his part-time job they were then able to make ends meet financially without going into debt.

Freedom, Not Force

The Johnsons tried to keep their advice as to their children's future vocations to a minimum. They naturally checked out the colleges they chose, and gave them needed guidance as to courses which would enable them to pursue their goals more quickly and suggestions for summer work which would aid them in preparing for a certain profession. They did not, however, nag their children into following their advice. They suggested a speed-reading course for Mike, who was a slow reader; additional music lessons for Scott in various instruments to increase his proficiency; a job in a dental lab for Tom to familiarize himself with the making of teeth; and the secretarial courses for Lynn. Their children usually took their advice as coming from the Lord, but never felt pressured to do so because they simply offered a suggestion and let it drop if there was no response from the young person. We can't choose the life work of our child, because he is an individual and must follow God's path for himself. Allow the Lord to lead your young people and guide them into the areas He chooses for them. This is where they will find fulfillment.

12

Prospective In-laws

Back in the days of the new swimming pool when the children were in grade school, Jim and Nancy would have been shocked at the thought that they were prospective in-laws. Although they assumed that all four of their children would be married some day, it seemed so far off that preparing to be "in-laws" didn't even enter their minds.

All Those "Mother-in-law Jokes"

Being an in-law requires walking a fine line between interfering and ignoring. Both of those are extremes and causes a breech in the relationship. Preparing for this difficult job begins in the dating days.

For instance, when Tom was dating Pat, whom he later married, Jim and Nancy had an opportunity to build a relationship with her before she became their daughter-in-law. They began looking at every girlfriend or boyfriend as a possible member of the family. They were warm, loving and open with her and made her feel welcome in their home. They encouraged Tommy to invite her to dinner and include her on weekend outings to their cabin or picnics to the beach. They didn't "push" him into bringing her along, but realized when he began spending all of his spare time with her that he was getting serious. He was young (20) and they felt deep down that it was a little soon for him to be taking on the responsibility of marriage, but after a man-to-man talk with his dad, they realized he wanted to be engaged to Pat.

Jim and Nancy gave their blessing because they realized that to oppose it would scar the relationship between them and the young couple. They loved Pat, she was a Christian, and their only reservation was their youth. They encouraged them to wait a year before marriage, which they did, and after the wedding, Pat continued to work and help Tom through his schooling. His parents contributed to his college education, too, as they would have done so had he not married. Pat had felt like "one of the family" for two years before they were married, so the adjustment to being in-laws was easy for all of them. Her family loved Tom, too, what with her brother being his best friend, so there were none of the problems that sometimes go with new relationships.

Two (Families) Become One

The Johnsons made it a point to get to know Pat's family as soon as it became apparent that Tom was serious about her. They had met them briefly before, but didn't know them in a personal way. Nancy Johnson invited them for dinner and their friendship bloomed. As they were choosing flowers for the wedding, giggling and obviously enjoying themselves, the florist remarked that it was very unusual to see two mothers-in-law having such a good time together. Her observation provided them with the opportunity to tell her that they were enjoying "Christian fellowship" and to witness to her.

If You Don't Like 'em, Don't Knock 'em

What if your son or daughter brings home a girl or boy of whom you disapprove? This didn't happen often in the Johnson household, but occasionally one of the children would begin dating someone their parents could see would bring them unhappiness. Usually it would be a person who was obviously selfish or egocentric or moody or bad-tempered or highly critical. Their method was to treat that person exactly the same as any other guest in their home. Then they would pray that God would reveal these negative qualities to their daughter or son. And they would never criticize the undesirable traits of the person. This would only have put their youngster on the defensive and given him closed ears to any further advice. They would often suggest that the person be invited for a weekend at their cabin. This would result in close contact over a two or three day period and by the end of that time, it was usually obvious that the personality did not fit in with the easygoing lifestyle of the Johnson family! Many a time, after dropping off the guest after one of these weekends, whoever brought him or her would remark, "Well! That's the end of that! What a bad temper!" Or, "Can you imagine a girl who was afraid to walk in the woods because of the dirt and bugs?" God was faithful to point out that this was not Mister or Miss "Right."

Get Acquainted

The Johnsons found it was easier to get to know Lynn's boyfriends than the boys' girlfriends. Boys usually spend their time at the girl's home, and a special effort has to be made to make the girl feel welcome at the boy's home. They overcame this by including the girlfriends on special family outings geared for the kids . . . like skiing, picnics, swim parties, barbecues, miniature golfing, etc. If one of the boys began dating a girl steadily, Jim and Nancy would invite them out for dinner at a restaurant with a fun activity afterward. This gave them an opportunity to observe the girl and helped her to open up and share with them. They encouraged the college-career group at church to meet at their home and for many years held one of the weekly Bible studies there. This drew them close to the young people and taught them how to communicate with that age group. They did not, themselves, attend the Bible study with the kids, but they provided the snacks afterward and were always available to talk with them.

Jim and Nancy shared their teenagers' enthusiasm for their boyfriends and girlfriends, and made an effort to notice the good points so they could intelligently comment on them. They also made sure to remember their names! Parents who ask "Is 'what's-his-name' coming over tonight?" will find communication pretty scarce with 'what's-his-name's' girlfriend! The Johnsons made friends with so many college age kids that after their own children were grown and married, they were often visited by these young men and women who introduced their husbands or wives and showed off new babies! Their love for these friends of their children was real, and there was no doubt about it.

Marrying Them Off

Tommy was the first one married in the family, followed by Lynn, then Scott, and lastly Mike, who was in his late twenties before he settled down. This was a blessing from God, who saw to it that he got his spiritual life in order before bringing him a wife.

Lynn's wedding, of course, was the most traumatic, because Nancy had to assume the full responsibility for planning it. She often remarked that being "Mother-of-the-Groom was fun," but the role of "Mother-of-the-Bride" was frustrating. (Until the wedding day, of course . . . then it was the most fun of all!) There were so many details to remember and Nancy was well aware of her sanguine temperament and tendency to forget things. She made lists, more lists, and lists of where to find her other lists!

Wedding Hints

The first thing Nancy and Lynn did after the wedding date was set was to buy a book called *Checklist for a Perfect Wedding*. This is an inexpensive paperback book available in any bookstore or department store. It has check lists and wedding etiquette and advice. Wedding etiquette is not so strict anymore, but both Ted and Lynn wanted a spiritual wedding which was more or less traditional.

It is important, first of all, to engage the church and minister, and the place for the reception. Everything else is built around that. The photographer was next . . . they become booked up very quickly if they are good, and the Johnsons felt that pictures were important. They later spent many happy hours looking at the children's wedding albums and reminiscing. The florist needs to be booked, too—and if your church has a wedding consultant, she will recommend several—and also someone to do the cake. Check with friends for suggestions on photographers, florists, bakers, caterers, etc. Those who have had experience putting on a wedding can not only offer suggestions as to the people with whom they were pleased, they can steer you clear of mistakes!

Some helpful hints from Nancy Johnson are as follows:

1. Do your own invitations. Lynn and Ted engaged their photographer to take them to some nearby woods to take pictures for the invitations. These are somewhat new, but becoming very popular. Friends and relatives love receiving a picture of the

engaged couple, and those from far away who can't make the wedding are doubly blessed. There is usually a close-up of the couple on the front . . . Ted and Lynn were shown leaning against an old picket fence with trees behind them. They also had a picture on the inside—opposite the worded invitation—showing them walking hand-in-hand down a path. Use your imagination. Most print shops will do these at a nominal cost, and there are even some where you can type the invitation on a script writer, saving the printing bill.

2. Print shops often have napkins and thank you notes available, too. Sometimes stationery shops will give you a discount on thank you notes when you buy them in quantity.

3. Try wholesale distributing companies for paper plates, cups, punch mix, and plastic forks and spoons. They will often sell them to the public at wholesale costs.

4. Rather than an expensive caterer, try hiring your church women's fellowship group or wedding committee. The money usually goes to the church, and it will not be as costly as professional services. You can keep your menu simple . . . sliced ham or turkey, salads, relishes, rolls. Lynn had a spring wedding and fresh fruit was in season, so there were punch bowls

full of melon balls, strawberries, grapes, sliced bananas and fresh pineapple. Deliciously sweet, it needed no dressing and was the hit of the buffet. It was purchased at a fruit stand at a lower price than in a supermarket.

5. Instead of traditional favors, Lynn and Ted had little scrolls tied with a ribbon which were given out to guests as they entered the church. On these scrolls was a printed note from Ted and Lynn thanking everyone for coming and telling of their commitment to Christ and to each other. Under their names were the words to a hymn of praise, which the wedding party and guests sang as the couple left the church during the recessional, instead of the traditional organ postlude. This was very effective and ended the wedding on a note of praise!

6. Because of the large crowd attending, guests were encouraged to go through the buffet line while the photographs were being taken. The reception line was held after the photographs, and some of the guests ate before the line and some after they went through it. The wedding party ate after the reception line, and an ice chest was packed for them by those preparing the food to take with them on their honeymoon. They had a lovely buffet

supper on·their balcony overlooking the ocean that evening.

7. For centerpieces for the tables, flowering plants were purchased and put into baskets covered with net and tied with ribbon. They were later planted in the yard. They were also used at the rehearsal dinner.

8. Ted's mother rented a recreation hall for the rehearsal dinner because of the many friends and relatives from out of town. A committee from her church prepared the food so she was able to enjoy the festivities. This, or a caterer, is much preferable to the cooking and serving being done by the groom's mother. This is one time to "splurge" and enjoy oneself.

Give It To The Lord and Enjoy It

These are only a few suggestions, but this is not meant to be a wedding planning book. The most important thing to remember about planning a wedding is to dedicate it to the Lord and ask Him to help you to remember all the details so that it will bring Him glory. God placed great importance on weddings in the Bible, and He would want them to be as nice as possible. Jesus performed His first miracle at a wedding.

The second most important point is to enjoy the occasion and the friends and relatives who gather to help you celebrate. A wedding should be fun . . . not a nerve-wracking, frustrating affair where everyone is jumping at everyone else. Relax and enjoy it, and don't worry! The Lord reminded Nancy Johnson of everything that was important, and the wedding was truly glorifying to the Lord.

Interfere Or Ignore?

And what about after the wedding? How often should you visit the newlyweds and when should you expect to see them? The Johnsons and Clarks (Ted's family) made it a point never to drop in unless they were invited, during the first year. If they hadn't seen the young couple for a week or so, they would call on the telephone to see how they were. They might add that when their calendar was free, they would like to have them to dinner. Lynn and Ted would check their schedule and make a date for dinner at one of the parents'. On most holidays, the parents, who had become good friends, would get together at one home and have potluck. They could easily accommodate a large crowd this way and it was no strain on any one person to do all the cooking.

'Twas the Night Before Christmas

Christmas can be a source of irritation in many a new marriage. Where should they spend it? At whose parents should they have dinner? If the parents get along well, these family potlucks can be the answer. In the case of both Ted's parents and Pat's (Tom's wife), they opened their gifts on Christmas morning. The young couples would spend that time with those parents and come Christmas eve to the Johnson's when they would open their gifts. Christmas dinner was held in the Johnson's cabin in the nearby mountains for all the families, with Nancy cooking the turkey and the others providing the trimmings. If this isn't practical in your family, ask the Lord to show you a way the holiday can be celebrated with the least inconvenience to anyone. If you feel nervous suggesting to your new in-laws that they spend Christmas dinner with you, just remember that they will probably heave a sigh of relief. They may be thinking the newlyweds will come to your house and they will be left out; or that they will come to theirs and hurt your feelings.

Turn The Other Cheek

If both families are Christians, there is usually no problem. However, if your child marries a Christian whose parents are not saved, it's liable to be another story. The best course to follow here is God's way. *You* do the giving in. If you have family traditions and so do they, and they seem not to want to come to a compromise, let them have their way. And go along with it graciously, not with a sour face and negative attitude. It's nice to have family traditions, but it's nicer to have family peace! What good are your traditions if you are forcing them upon your child's in-laws? You will only alienate the new relatives, make things uncomfortable for your child and cause him to have a problem in his marriage. If he goes along with his wife's parents to please her, and you make sure he knows how hurt you are, he will have guilt feelings. If he insists on doing things your way, he will hurt his wife and her parents. He's caught in a bind. If you give in, graciously, you will prove to your children that you live your Christianity and it will be a wonderful witness to those in-laws for whose conversion you have undoubtedly been praying. If you react the way God wants, He will bless you!

Untie The Apron Strings!

There is no way you can be good in-laws and not untie those apron strings. When your child marries, he is told in the Bible to leave his parents and cling to his wife (Genesis 2:24) and you need to help him to do this. Tom and Pat were in another state going to school and the independence was good for them. At a very young age, Tom learned to manage money, take care of his wife and home, and later, when that first grandchild arrived, undertook the responsibility of being a father as if he had been born to it. His parents were there when he needed help, but they never interfered with his decisions or the way he handled his family. He was head of his house, just as his father was, and the Lord was his source of guidance. Being an "in-law" can be a wonderful experience; your children's marriages need not make your family smaller . . . it can make it bigger and "double the pleasure, double the fun!"

13

Don't Preach It
. . . Live It!

Jim Johnson was talking to his neighbor, Stan, out in the yard. Stan was a Christian, but had not committed his life completely to the Lord. He felt that believing Christ died for his sins and attending church on Sundays was enough to get to Heaven and anything beyond that bordered on the fanatic. He was complaining about his children as he watched Jim trim his hedge. "No matter how often I tell them they shouldn't drink, they still come home drunk on Saturday nights!'' Jim glanced at the martini in Stan's hand, but said nothing. ''And the way they drive . . . I have enough problems paying my own speeding tickets without adding theirs to the bill!''

Don't Do As I Say . . . Do As I Do

Jim could finally stand it no longer. At the risk of offending his neighbor he said, ''Well, we've found in our family that our kids listen a lot more to what we *do* than what we *say*. If we don't back up our standards by our own example, they feel it really isn't very important to us.'' Stan's face reddened and he seemed embarrassed by the drink in his hand. ''Yeah . . . I guess I see what you mean. 'Don't do as I do . . . do as I say' doesn't have much influence, does it?''

Later as Jim was sharing what happened with Nancy, she agreed with his response to Stan. ''I remember how he was over here lambasting the government and calling the president names, and then was furious when his son refused to register for the draft. And Joan, his wife, complains constantly about the risqué way their daughter dresses; yet, I've seen *her* at the grocery store in short shorts and a brief halter top that she wears sunbathing. She said she didn't feel like changing before she shopped. The girl is just following her mother's example.''

It is true that your children learn more by

your example than by your words. They tend to forget words, but pictures stay in their minds. The way you live makes a lasting impression on them that they will carry around their whole lives.

Your Life Is Their Textbook

And how do you live? Do you take time each day to be in the Word and have your personal devotions? Are you involved in your church . . . not just attending on Sunday, but serving the Lord in your own special spot? Jim and Nancy Johnson were both members of the Calling Club in their church, calling on those who had visited. Jim was an elder and also taught a Bible Study in their home for couples, each week. Nancy taught a Ladies' Bible Study at the church one morning a week. This required disciplined study on both their parts, which was good for their children to observe. Jim commuted to work in his car, and listened to Bible tapes and sermons as he drove. If the children used his car and pushed the button to hear a tape, they would find themselves listening to Scripture, sermons or Christian music. They knew their parents' commitment to Christ was not just a "Sunday Church" type thing . . . it was as much a part of their daily lives as eating or breathing.

Scott often told of the time he went out for the evening but decided to come home early to do some studying. Not wanting to interrupt his parents who were still at the dinner table with guests, he let himself quietly in the side door and went to his room. Shortly, he heard his dad telling the non-Christian couple what Jesus Christ meant in his life and to that of his family. As his father continued to witness to the couple and answer their questions, Scott quietly listened to him in his room. "I realized then," he said, "that my parents were no different when they were with non-Christians with none of us kids around than when they have our pastor to dinner. They really *live* their Christianity!"

What would your children hear in like circumstances? Would they come home to everyone being a little tipsy on the dinner wine and laughing at off-color jokes? Or gossiping about friends who are not present? Would you have to worry about what they might have heard? If so, perhaps you had better take another look at your priorities.

Number One

Is Jesus Christ *really* number one in your life? When our Christian young men were in Viet Nam and the villagers would see a cross around their necks, they would say "Number One" in English as they pointed to it. If Christ is "number one" in your life there should be no doubt about it. If you were about to be sentenced for being a Christian, would there be enough evidence in your life to convict you? You can be a Christian without a total commitment, but you can't have the abundant life! You can't have God's perfect plan for your life! And your faith will not grow. Faith comes from hearing and hearing by the Word of God! (Romans 10:17) If you're not in the Word of God, how can you have faith? If you need to make this total commitment . . . dedicate yourself and all you have to the Lord . . . don't put it off any longer. You are only putting off God's blessing if you do!

To Grandmother's House We Go!

One area where many parents fall down is in communication with grandparents. They are too likely to use them as convenient baby-sitters, but not really include them in their lives. They go to dinner and then leave. They accept their gifts but exclude them from their activities. If your parents are in good health, take them with you for that picnic or family weekend in the mountains. Not that they should *always* be included in everything, but do it often enough so your children can grow to appreciate them as personalities.

The Johnsons often visited with their parents and always invited them for holidays. The children liked and respected their grandparents and loved staying with them. Grandpa Johnson had a small farm in a town close by, and was a favorite with all the grandchildren. He had a wealth of stories to tell, and Grandma Johnson was the best "baker" in the county. Their "little country church" was fun for the children and they learned how close people in the country can be to each other. Nancy's parents were "city folk" and a visit with them always meant the zoo or dinner at the newest restaurant in town, and when the children were small, a visit to the biggest toy department they had ever seen! And lots of Christian stories read to them until they were old enough to read and discuss the Bible themselves.

Best of all, there was always a listening ear to *whatever* the children had to say. If it was a problem, there was sympathy and good advice; if it was a joy, every detail was listened to and the proper questions asked. Interest and love was apparent and both Jim and Nancy were grateful for their wonderful parents. They had taught them through their lives how to live before their own children.

14

Pray, Play
and Stay Together

Family closeness doesn't just "happen"
. . . it takes time, the sacrifice of some of our
own interests, and most of all, guidance from
the Lord. When asked, after their family was
grown, how they all turned out so well and
remained in their close bond of love, Jim
Johnson had a few words of advice.

Pray

"First of all, the most important lesson we ever learned from our own parents was to pray together. They always prayed with us, and we always prayed with our own children. We were able to be so much more open with each other because we were open with God. We never ate a meal, went on a journey, had a problem to discuss or went to sleep without praying. We asked God's guidance in everything we did, and encouraged our children to do the same.

"There were times when we didn't pray enough or failed to pray before some event or test, and we always knew it. Things just didn't work out the same as when we remembered to pray. I remember Tommy's senior year on the football team; we prayed before every game that God would protect them and prevent them from receiving any serious injuries. They not only won every game that year . . . the most serious injury of the season was a dislocated knee one boy got from horsing around in the locker room!"

Play

The second most important thing they did was to play together. Jim said he worked with too many men who never had time to play touch football with his boys or take them fishing or teach them to swim, but had time to play at least 36 holes of golf each week! He determined not to be that kind of father. Many fathers give their sons money but not time, and mothers are too busy pursuing careers of their own to bother with their daughter's needs. Some families even take separate vacations . . . the father going on a hunting trip with the men, the mother to a resort, while the children are left with babysitters. Not that parents shouldn't get away by themselves occasionally, but do you realize you're going to have 25 years or so to do things without the kids after they are grown?

Building Family Traditions

"We talked about family traditions," continued Jim, "and I guess we had quite a few of those. You always think of traditions as things like having oyster stew on Christmas Eve and cutting your own Christmas tree and decorating it a certain way, but they're more than that. It was our family tradition to have Proverbs for dessert, and it was another tradition to go to my brother's cabin on a lake in another state for vacations. We would camp on the way there and back, and take as many kids as the car would hold. As the kids got into late high school and early college, we took more than one car so we could take more people. One year we took a friend each for Mike, Lynn and Scott and Tom joined us a couple of days later with five of his boyfriends! We had a boat for water skiing, and there was swimming, horseback riding, hiking, fishing—with all the nieces and nephews—and a great time was had by all. Our grown-up kids look back on those times now as the best they ever had.''

''We had our holiday traditions, too,'' Nancy joined in. ''We always put our turkey in the oven and went to the Homecoming Football game at the high school. We had dinner after the game. Christmas has always been spent at our mountain cabin. It's big enough for lots of extra people, and we all look forward to at least a week up there at Christmas. We go out in the woods and chop our own tree (with permission from a friend who has some acreage) and decorate it with special ornaments . . . either homemade, purchased in far away places on vacations, or things given to us by grandparents. Everything has a special meaning. When the kids were little and believed in Santa Claus, we opened our presents on Christmas morning. As they got older, they didn't want to wait until morning, so we open them around 10:00 p.m. after spending time in the Word and reading the Christmas story from Luke, and praying. We have a big fire in the fireplace and we each take turns opening one gift while the others watch. That way we have the joy of seeing our gift to each person opened and it drags it out so it takes a long time. We even trained our dog to wait his turn to chew open his presents of doggie treats and playthings.''

Families Are Fun!

''Another kind of silly thing we did which

got to be a family tradition," said Jim, "was to give ourselves crazy names when we were camping. That's the only time we used them, but how we laughed over them! My name was "Harvey" and Nancy's was "Maude." Tommy was "Basil" and Mike, "Hector," Lynn was "Abigail" and Scott was "Aloysius." When we'd call the kids to come for dinner, the people camping around us would give us weird looks at the unusual names. Even now, the kids will call us "Harvey and Maude" once in awhile and start everyone reminiscing over those camping trips. If we took anyone with us, we gave them names, too, so they could join in the fun! It's the kind of thing that isn't particularly funny to anyone else but can send the family into whoops of laughter!

"Another thing we always did," continued Jim, "was 'make up and add to.' For instance, one time we read an article in the newspaper about some college boys who lived on dog food for two months to see which brand was best. Nancy wondered if they had any ill effects, and Scott replied, 'No . . . but they ate their dinner under the table from then on.' 'And they turned around in circles and scrunched up their covers before they went to bed at night,' added Tom. 'And they chased the mail man!' Lynn put in. 'And they had to wear flea collars,' Mike continued.

"This would go on and on with each person adding more until we all had stomachaches from laughing. That's one thing we always had plenty of in our family . . . laughter!''

God is the center of the Johnson family and all their offspring. Tom and Pat and their Clint, and his new baby sister; Mike and his bride, Diane; Lynn and Ted and their twins, and Scott and Janey. Jim and Nancy can look back on the years of a growing family as filled with love and laughter, with a few sprinklings of heartaches, but always with Christ as the Cornerstone. Every family has a story, but with Jesus Christ, you can be sure it will be a ''love story.''